Navigation

Part I: Foundations of Bond Inve.

   1. Introduction to the Bond Market................................ 1

   2. Bond Fund Basics 12

   3. Bond ETF Basics 22

Part II: Navigating the Bond Fund Landscape.................. 33

   4. Active vs. Passive Bond Management....................... 33

   5. Short-Term vs. Long-Term Bond Funds 41

   6. High-Yield vs. Investment-Grade Bond Funds 49

   7. Municipal Bond Funds: Tax Advantages and Considerations... 57

   8. Government Bond Funds: Stability and Security 64

   9. Corporate Bond Funds: Diversification and Sector Exposure 72

   10. International Bond Funds: Global Diversification.. 80

Part III: Evaluating and Selecting Bond Funds and ETFs 87

   11. Bond Fund Expenses and Fees 87

   12. Bond Fund Performance Analysis 95

   13. Bond Fund Ratings and Research 102

   14. Bond Fund Dividends and Distributions 109

   15. Building a Bond Portfolio with ETFs and Funds.. 116

Part IV: Advanced Strategies and Considerations 124

   16. Using Bond Funds and ETFs in Retirement Planning 124

   17. Bond Funds and ETFs for Specific Financial Goals 133

   18. The Future of Bond Funds and ETFs.................... 141

Part I: Foundations of Bond Investing

1. Introduction to the Bond Market

Understanding Bonds: Basics of Issuance, Maturity, and Yield

Bonds, often called **fixed-income securities**, represent a loan you make to a borrower—typically a government or corporation. This loan agreement outlines specific terms, including the amount borrowed (the **principal**), the interest rate (the **coupon rate**), and the repayment date (the **maturity date**). Understanding these core elements is crucial for navigating the world of bond investing.

The *issuance* process involves the borrower selling bonds to raise capital. These bonds are typically offered through investment banks or underwriters who manage the sale and distribution to investors. The issuance price can vary based on market conditions and investor demand. A bond issued at a price above its face value is sold at a *premium*, while one issued below its face value is sold at a *discount*.

The **maturity date** signifies the date on which the borrower promises to repay the principal to the bondholder. Bonds are categorized by their maturity lengths: *short-term* bonds typically mature within one to three years, *intermediate-term* bonds mature in three to ten years, and *long-term* bonds mature in more than ten years. The maturity date significantly influences a bond's sensitivity to interest rate changes; longer-term bonds generally exhibit greater sensitivity.

The **yield** represents the return an investor receives from a bond. It's expressed as a percentage and reflects the combination of the coupon rate and any capital gains or losses from price fluctuations. The *coupon rate* is the annual interest payment expressed as a percentage of the bond's face value, paid regularly (e.g., semi-annually) until maturity. However, the **current yield** is calculated based on the bond's current market price, providing a more accurate picture of the return an investor will receive if they buy the bond at its current market price. The **yield to maturity (YTM)** takes into account the bond's current price, coupon payments, and the difference between the current price and the face value at maturity to provide a more comprehensive measure of a bond's total return.

For instance, a *corporate bond* might have a **face value** of $1,000, a **coupon rate** of 5%, and a **maturity date** of five years. This means the bondholder receives $50 in interest annually ($1000 x 0.05). However, if the bond trades at $950 in the secondary market, the current yield and YTM will be higher than 5% because of the discount. The interplay between these three key elements – issuance, maturity, and yield – determines the risk and reward profile of any given bond, making understanding these concepts essential for successful bond investing.

In summary, understanding the issuance process, the maturity date, and yield calculations is fundamental for effective bond investment strategies. By carefully examining these elements, investors can make informed decisions about which bonds align with their risk tolerance and financial objectives.

Types of Bonds: Government, Corporate, Municipal

The bond market offers a diverse range of investment opportunities, broadly categorized into three main types: government bonds, corporate bonds, and municipal bonds. Each type possesses unique characteristics regarding risk, return, and tax implications, making it crucial for investors to understand their differences before making investment decisions.

Government Bonds: The Foundation of Stability

Government bonds, issued by national or local governments, represent the bedrock of fixed-income investments. These bonds are generally considered low-risk investments because they're backed by the full faith and credit of the issuing government. A government's ability to tax its citizens and manage its economy generally ensures repayment. However, the return on government bonds is typically lower than other bond types due to this lower perceived risk.

Examples include:

- **Treasury bonds (T-bonds):** Issued by the U.S. Treasury, these are considered the safest bonds available. They have maturities ranging from 10 to 30 years.
- **Treasury notes (T-notes):** Also issued by the U.S. Treasury, these have maturities ranging from 2 to 10 years.

- **Treasury bills (T-bills):** Short-term debt securities with maturities of less than a year.
- **Agency bonds:** Issued by government-sponsored enterprises (GSEs) like Fannie Mae and Freddie Mac, these are generally considered very safe, though not as safe as direct Treasury securities.

The relative safety of government bonds makes them a cornerstone of many *conservative investment portfolios*.

Corporate Bonds: Navigating the Corporate World

Corporate bonds are issued by companies to raise capital for various purposes, such as expansion, acquisitions, or refinancing. Unlike government bonds, the risk associated with corporate bonds is significantly higher because their repayment depends on the financial health and stability of the issuing corporation. Consequently, corporate bonds generally offer higher yields than government bonds to compensate investors for this increased risk.

These bonds can be further categorized by their credit rating:

- **Investment-grade bonds:** Rated Baa3/BBB- or higher by credit rating agencies (e.g., Moody's, S&P, Fitch), these bonds are considered relatively safe.
- **High-yield bonds (junk bonds):** Rated below Baa3/BBB-, these bonds carry significantly higher default risk but offer higher yields to compensate investors for the increased risk.

Investing in corporate bonds requires a careful assessment of the issuer's financial strength, industry prospects, and overall market conditions. Diversification across different corporations and industries is crucial to mitigate risk.

Municipal Bonds: A Tax-Advantaged Option

Municipal bonds are issued by state and local governments to finance public projects, such as schools, hospitals, and infrastructure improvements. A key advantage of municipal bonds is their tax-exempt status. The interest earned on most municipal bonds is exempt from federal income tax, and often from state and local taxes as well. This makes them particularly attractive to investors in higher tax brackets.

However, municipal bonds are not entirely risk-free. The creditworthiness of the issuing municipality is crucial, and the risk of default is always present, although typically lower than with corporate bonds. Different types of municipal bonds include:

- **General obligation bonds (GO bonds):** Backed by the full taxing power of the municipality.
- **Revenue bonds:** Backed by the revenue generated by the project being financed.

Careful due diligence and understanding of the issuer's financial health are essential before investing in municipal bonds.

Understanding the nuances of each bond type—government, corporate, and municipal—is fundamental to building a well-diversified and effective bond portfolio. The risk-return profile of each differs significantly, necessitating a thorough assessment of individual investor needs and risk tolerance. This understanding empowers informed decision-making, leading to better outcomes within the context of a comprehensive investment strategy.

Bond Market Risks: Interest Rate Risk, Inflation Risk, Default Risk

Investing in bonds, whether through individual bonds or bond funds/ETFs, inherently involves risk. Understanding these risks is crucial for making informed investment decisions and managing your portfolio effectively. Three primary risks dominate the bond market landscape: interest rate risk, inflation risk, and default risk. Let's delve into each one.

Interest Rate Risk: The Yield Curve's Shadow

Interest rate risk is perhaps the most significant concern for bond investors. It stems from the inverse relationship between bond prices and interest rates. When interest rates rise, the value of existing bonds with lower coupon rates declines, as newly issued bonds offer higher yields. Conversely, when interest rates fall, the value of existing bonds increases. This fluctuation can significantly impact the returns of your bond investments, especially for bonds with longer maturities or lower coupon payments. The *duration* of a bond—a measure of its price sensitivity to interest rate changes—is a critical factor in assessing this risk. Longer-duration bonds are more vulnerable to interest rate hikes than shorter-duration bonds. Sophisticated investors use tools like duration analysis and strategies like laddering (investing in bonds with staggered maturities) to mitigate interest rate risk. Understanding the yield curve, which illustrates the relationship between bond yields and maturities, is essential for navigating the dynamics of interest rate risk. A steep yield curve often signals expectations of future interest rate increases, which could negatively affect bond prices.

Inflation Risk: The Erosion of Purchasing Power

Inflation, the persistent increase in the general price level of goods and services, poses a serious threat to the real return of bond investments. While bonds offer a fixed income stream, the purchasing power of those future payments can be eroded by inflation. High inflation diminishes the value of future cash flows, reducing the real return of your bonds. To combat this risk, investors often consider bonds with inflation-linked features, such as Treasury Inflation-Protected Securities (TIPS). These securities adjust their principal value based on the Consumer Price Index (CPI), offering a hedge against inflation. However, even TIPS don't offer complete protection, as inflation expectations can be volatile and difficult to predict precisely. Careful consideration of your investment timeframe and inflation forecasts is essential for managing this critical risk.

Default Risk: The Specter of Non-Payment

Default risk, also known as credit risk, refers to the possibility that the bond issuer will fail to make timely interest payments or repay the principal amount at maturity. This risk is inherent in corporate bonds and municipal bonds. The likelihood of default varies depending on the creditworthiness of the issuer. Credit rating agencies, such as Moody's, S&P, and Fitch, assign ratings to bonds based on their assessment of the issuer's financial strength and ability to meet its obligations. **Higher-rated bonds (investment-grade)** generally carry lower default risk, while lower-rated bonds (high-yield or junk bonds) offer higher yields to compensate for the increased risk of default. Diversification across different issuers and credit ratings is a key strategy for managing default risk. Thorough due diligence, including analyzing the issuer's financial statements and industry conditions, is vital in assessing the potential for default.

In conclusion, navigating the bond market requires a thorough understanding of interest rate risk, inflation risk, and default risk. These risks are interconnected and influence investment decisions. Employing strategies such as diversification, duration management, and careful issuer selection allows investors to mitigate these risks and improve the chances of achieving their financial objectives. Remember that seeking professional financial advice can further enhance your ability to manage these risks within your specific investment context. Don't hesitate to consult with qualified advisors to tailor a bond strategy aligned with your personal risk tolerance and financial goals.

The Role of Bonds in a Diversified Portfolio

In the dynamic world of investing, diversification is paramount. A well-constructed portfolio isn't just about maximizing returns; it's about mitigating risk. While stocks often take center stage, owing to their potential for significant growth, they also carry substantial volatility. This is where bonds, often considered the *bedrock of stability*, step in to play a crucial role. Bonds, with their relatively lower risk profile, offer a vital counterbalance to the inherent fluctuations of equities, creating a more resilient and balanced investment strategy. The incorporation of bonds into a diversified portfolio isn't simply a matter of adding another asset class; it's a strategic maneuver designed to enhance the overall portfolio's performance and resilience in the face of market downturns.

The primary function of bonds in a diversified portfolio is risk reduction. Unlike stocks, which represent ownership in a company and are thus subject to the fortunes (and misfortunes) of that particular entity, bonds represent a loan to an issuer (be it a government, corporation, or municipality). This debt obligation means that bondholders are entitled to periodic interest payments and the eventual repayment of the principal. While bond prices can fluctuate – particularly in response to interest rate changes – their volatility generally lags behind that of stocks. This inherent stability makes bonds effective shock absorbers during periods of market stress. When stock prices plummet, the relative stability of bonds can help cushion the overall portfolio's losses.

Furthermore, bonds contribute to portfolio diversification by offering a different correlation profile to stocks. Stock and bond returns often move independently, meaning that when one asset class experiences declines, the other may not necessarily follow suit. This lack of perfect correlation is a powerful tool for reducing overall portfolio risk. Consider a scenario where the stock market experiences a significant correction. A portfolio heavily invested in stocks will likely suffer substantial losses. However, a portfolio that includes a substantial bond allocation will experience a significantly smaller decline, thanks to the bonds' counterbalancing effect.

The optimal allocation of bonds within a portfolio depends on several factors, including the investor's risk tolerance, investment time horizon, and financial goals. Younger investors with longer time horizons might opt for a smaller bond allocation, allowing them to take on more risk in pursuit of higher potential returns. Conversely, investors closer to retirement, with a shorter time horizon and a greater need for capital preservation, will likely favor a larger bond allocation to minimize potential losses. A well-defined investment strategy should carefully assess these variables and construct a portfolio that aligns with the investor's specific circumstances.

Beyond risk reduction and diversification, bonds also provide a steady stream of income. The regular interest payments received from bonds can supplement an investor's income, particularly valuable during retirement or periods of market uncertainty. This predictable income stream contrasts with the more unpredictable dividend payouts from stocks, offering a reliable source of cash flow that can be used for living expenses or reinvestment.

However, it's crucial to understand that bonds are not without risk. Interest rate risk, inflation risk, and credit risk all pose potential threats to bond investments. Interest rate risk refers to the inverse relationship between bond prices and interest rates: as interest rates rise, bond prices generally fall, and vice-versa. Inflation risk threatens the purchasing power of future bond payments, while credit risk represents the possibility of a bond issuer defaulting on its obligations. Careful selection of bonds, considering factors such as maturity, credit rating, and issuer, is therefore essential to mitigate these risks.

In conclusion, bonds play a multifaceted role in a well-diversified portfolio. They act as a powerful buffer against market volatility, reducing overall portfolio risk and enhancing stability. The regular income stream generated by bonds provides financial security, supplementing other income sources. While not without their own risks, bonds offer a crucial element of balance, helping investors navigate the complexities of the investment landscape and pursue their financial objectives with a greater degree of confidence and resilience. A thoughtful allocation of bonds, tailored to individual circumstances and risk tolerance, remains a cornerstone of successful long-term investing.

2. Bond Fund Basics

What are Bond Funds?

Bond funds, also known as bond mutual funds, are investment vehicles that pool money from multiple investors to purchase a diversified portfolio of bonds. Unlike owning individual bonds, which can be cumbersome and require significant capital, bond funds offer a convenient and accessible way to gain exposure to the bond market. Think of them as a basket containing various types of bonds, each contributing to the overall fund's performance and risk profile.

The core objective of a bond fund is to generate income for its investors through interest payments made by the bonds held within the portfolio. These interest payments, known as dividends, are typically distributed to fund shareholders periodically, often on a monthly or quarterly basis. However, it's important to note that while income generation is a primary goal, the fund's value can also fluctuate based on the market price of the underlying bonds.

The diversity offered by bond funds is a key advantage. A single bond fund can hold hundreds or even thousands of different bonds, issued by various governments, corporations, and municipalities. This diversification helps mitigate risk. If one bond in the portfolio defaults, the impact on the overall fund's value is likely to be minimal compared to the impact of a single bond default on an individual investor.

Bond funds are managed by professional fund managers who actively select and trade bonds to achieve the fund's investment objective. These managers make decisions about which bonds to buy or sell, aiming to maximize returns while managing risk. The level of management can vary significantly; some funds are actively managed, where the managers actively try to outperform the market, while others are passively managed, tracking a specific bond index and aiming to match its performance.

There's a wide range of bond funds catering to different investor needs and risk tolerances. Some funds focus on short-term bonds, which are less sensitive to interest rate fluctuations, while others invest in long-term bonds, offering higher potential returns but with greater interest rate risk. Other specialized bond funds may target specific sectors, such as high-yield corporate bonds (also known as junk bonds), municipal bonds, or government bonds. The choice of a suitable bond fund depends greatly on individual investor goals, risk appetite, and investment timeline.

Investing in bond funds involves fees, which are typically expressed as an expense ratio. These fees cover the costs of managing the fund, including the fund manager's salary, administrative expenses, and trading costs. It's crucial to compare the expense ratios of different bond funds before investing, as even small differences can significantly impact long-term returns.

In summary, bond funds offer a powerful tool for investors seeking to diversify their portfolios, generate income, and manage risk. By carefully considering your investment objectives and risk tolerance, you can choose a bond fund that aligns with your individual financial goals.

Remember to always conduct thorough research and understand the fund's investment strategy and associated fees before committing your capital.

Advantages and Disadvantages of Bond Funds

Bond funds, offering a diversified approach to fixed-income investing, present a compelling alternative to investing in individual bonds. However, like any investment vehicle, they come with their own set of advantages and disadvantages. Understanding these nuances is crucial for making informed investment decisions aligned with your financial goals and risk tolerance.

Advantages of Bond Funds:

- **Diversification:** This is arguably the most significant advantage. Bond funds pool money from multiple investors to purchase a diverse portfolio of bonds, mitigating the risk associated with investing in a single bond. This diversification spreads risk across various issuers, maturities, and credit qualities, reducing the impact of any individual bond's default or underperformance.

- **Professional Management:** Experienced fund managers handle the selection, purchasing, and selling of bonds within the fund. They leverage their expertise in fixed-income markets to make strategic decisions aimed at maximizing returns while managing risk effectively. This relieves individual investors of the burden of researching and managing a bond portfolio themselves.

- **Liquidity:** Unlike individual bonds, which can be illiquid and difficult to sell quickly, bond fund shares can generally be bought and sold easily on any trading day. This liquidity allows investors to access their funds relatively quickly when needed.
- **Affordability:** Bond funds offer accessibility to a wide range of bonds, even those with high minimum investment requirements. Investors can participate in the bond market with relatively small initial investments, making it more accessible than direct bond ownership.
- **Automatic Reinvestment of Income:** Many bond funds automatically reinvest dividend and interest payments, allowing investors to benefit from compounding returns. This feature simplifies the process of accumulating wealth over the long term.
- **Transparency:** Investors have access to regular reports and fund fact sheets that provide details about the fund's holdings, performance, and expenses. This allows them to monitor their investment and assess its performance against their expectations.
- Variety of Choices: The bond fund market offers a wide range of choices catering to different investment styles and objectives. Whether you prefer short-term, long-term, high-yield, or investment-grade bonds, you can find a fund that aligns with your specific needs.

Disadvantages of Bond Funds:

- *Fees and Expenses:* Bond funds charge management fees and expense ratios, which can eat into your returns over time. It's essential to compare the expense ratios of different funds before investing to minimize these costs.

- *Fluctuations in Net Asset Value (NAV):* While generally less volatile than equity funds, bond funds' NAVs can still fluctuate based on interest rate changes and the creditworthiness of the underlying bonds. This means your investment's value can go down as well as up.
- *Tax Implications:* Bond fund distributions are often taxable, adding another layer of complexity to your investment strategy. Capital gains distributions can affect your overall tax liability.
- *Lack of Control:* You don't have direct control over the specific bonds held within the fund. You rely on the fund manager's decisions regarding the portfolio's composition.
- *Potential for Manager Underperformance:* Active bond funds rely on the skill of the fund manager. If the manager makes poor investment choices, the fund's performance may lag behind the benchmark.
- *Limited Transparency in Active Management:* While fund fact sheets provide information, the precise decision-making process of active managers may not be entirely transparent.
- <u>Market Risk:</u> Although bond funds are generally considered less risky than equity funds, they are still subject to market fluctuations and interest rate risks. Rising interest rates can negatively impact the value of existing bonds in the portfolio.

In conclusion, bond funds offer a range of benefits, particularly diversification and professional management, but investors must carefully weigh the potential disadvantages, such as fees, lack of control, and the impact of interest rate changes before making an investment decision. Understanding the specific characteristics of different types of bond funds is crucial for selecting the one that best aligns with individual investor's risk tolerance and financial goals.

Types of Bond Fund Structures (Open-End, Closed-End)

The world of bond funds presents a diverse landscape of investment vehicles, and understanding their underlying structures is crucial for making informed investment decisions. Two primary structures dominate the market: *open-end* and *closed-end* funds. Each possesses unique characteristics that significantly impact investor experience and potential returns.

Open-end funds, often referred to as mutual funds, are the more common type. These funds continuously issue and redeem shares directly from the fund company. This means investors can buy shares whenever the fund is open for trading, and sell them back to the fund at the end of each trading day at the Net Asset Value (NAV). The NAV is calculated daily based on the market value of the bonds held within the fund. Because of this continuous creation and redemption of shares, the supply of shares is always flexible, adapting to investor demand. This flexibility makes open-end funds highly liquid, allowing investors relatively easy access to their money. However, this constant flow of money can sometimes impact the fund's ability to implement long-term investment strategies efficiently. Open-end funds are generally preferred by investors seeking regular access to their money and ease of entry and exit.

In contrast, **closed-end funds** operate differently. These funds issue a fixed number of shares during an initial public offering (IPO). Once all shares are sold, the fund company no longer issues or redeems shares. Investors seeking to buy shares must purchase them on the secondary market, typically through a stock exchange. This means the price of a closed-end fund's shares can fluctuate throughout the day, trading above or below its NAV, unlike open-end funds which always trade at NAV. This price discrepancy, known as the premium or discount to NAV, is influenced by market sentiment and investor demand. The fixed number of shares means closed-end funds may offer greater stability and predictability in managing their assets. They might pursue more long-term investment strategies not possible with open-end funds due to continuous share fluctuations. However, the relative lack of liquidity – meaning difficulty in buying or selling shares quickly – makes them a less suitable choice for investors who require frequent access to their capital. *Closed-end funds can be a suitable choice for long-term investors comfortable with fluctuating share prices and less liquidity.*

The choice between open-end and closed-end bond funds hinges significantly on individual investment goals, risk tolerance, and liquidity needs. Open-end funds offer unparalleled convenience and liquidity, while closed-end funds might provide opportunities for accessing specific market segments or leveraging the expertise of a seasoned fund manager in a more consistent, long-term strategy. A thorough understanding of these structural differences is paramount for investors to align their investment strategy with the appropriate fund structure.

Beyond the core differences in share issuance and trading mechanisms, investors should also consider the management styles, fee structures, and investment objectives of both open-end and closed-end bond funds. These factors, in conjunction with the structural aspects, collectively determine the suitability of a particular fund for a specific investor's profile. Careful research and consideration are essential for maximizing returns and minimizing risk in the bond market.

Ultimately, the decision rests on an investor's individual circumstances and financial objectives. Both open-ended and closed-ended structures offer unique advantages and disadvantages, which should be carefully weighed before committing investments.

Understanding Fund Prospectuses and Fact Sheets

Prospectuses and fact sheets are **crucial documents** for any investor considering a bond fund. They are not light reading, but taking the time to understand their contents is essential for making informed investment decisions. Think of them as your roadmap to navigating the complexities of the fund's investment strategy, fees, and risks. Ignoring them can lead to costly surprises down the line.

A *fund prospectus* is a comprehensive legal document that provides a detailed overview of the fund. It's the most complete source of information you will find. Expect it to be lengthy – often dozens of pages. It's designed to provide full transparency, covering everything from the fund's investment objectives and strategies to its risk factors and fee structure. Key sections to focus on include:

- **Investment Objective:** This section clearly states the fund's primary goal. Is it focused on capital appreciation, income generation, or a blend of both?

Understanding this objective is crucial for determining if the fund aligns with your personal investment goals.

- **Investment Strategy:** This explains how the fund manager intends to achieve the investment objective. Does the fund primarily invest in government bonds, corporate bonds, or a mix? What is their approach to managing risk? Are they actively managing the portfolio or following a passive index-tracking strategy?

- **Risk Factors:** This section outlines the potential risks associated with investing in the fund. These can range from interest rate risk and inflation risk to credit risk and liquidity risk. A thorough understanding of these risks is paramount before investing.

- **Fees and Expenses:** This is a critical section to scrutinize carefully. The prospectus will detail all fees charged, including management fees, expense ratios, and any other applicable charges. Compare these fees to those of similar funds to ensure you're getting a competitive rate.

- **Performance Information (Past Performance):** While past performance isn't indicative of future results, reviewing historical performance can provide insights into the fund's track record. Pay attention to the fund's consistency over various market conditions.

- **Financial Statements:** The prospectus will include the fund's financial statements, providing a snapshot of its assets, liabilities, and performance. While you may not need to pore over every detail, understanding the key figures can offer valuable insights into the fund's health.

A *fact sheet*, on the other hand, is a shorter, more concise summary of the key information found in the prospectus. It's a great starting point for quickly getting an overview of the fund. However, never rely solely on a fact sheet. It's designed to be a high-level summary, not a substitute for the detailed information provided in the prospectus.

Both prospectuses and fact sheets are **essential tools** for making informed investment decisions. By carefully reviewing these documents, you can gain a clearer understanding of the fund's objectives, strategies, risks, and fees, enabling you to assess whether it's a suitable addition to your portfolio. Don't hesitate to seek professional financial advice if you have any questions or uncertainties about the information contained within these important documents. Your financial well-being depends on it.

3. Bond ETF Basics

What are Bond ETFs?

Bond exchange-traded funds (ETFs) are investment vehicles that offer investors diversified exposure to a portfolio of bonds, all within a single, easily tradable security. Unlike individual bonds, which require purchasing and holding individual debt instruments, bond ETFs provide a convenient and cost-effective way to gain access to a broad range of fixed-income securities. They are traded throughout the day on stock exchanges, just like stocks, offering flexibility and liquidity that traditional bond mutual funds often lack.

At their core, bond ETFs are baskets of bonds that are passively managed to track a specific bond index or actively managed to achieve a particular investment objective. Passive bond ETFs aim to mirror the performance of a particular benchmark index, such as the Barclays Aggregate Bond Index or the iShares Core U.S. Aggregate Bond ETF (AGG), offering broad market exposure with low fees. Active bond ETFs, on the other hand, are managed by professional portfolio managers who actively select bonds based on their assessment of market conditions, seeking to outperform a benchmark index.

The transparency of bond ETFs is a significant advantage. Investors can readily view the underlying holdings of the ETF, providing complete transparency into the composition of their investment. This contrasts with some mutual funds, where the precise holdings may not be disclosed as frequently. This increased transparency allows investors to make more informed decisions about their investment strategies.

One of the key benefits of bond ETFs is their low expense ratios. Because they are often passively managed and trade on exchanges, their operating costs are generally lower than those of actively managed bond mutual funds. This translates to potentially higher returns for investors over the long term. The lower cost structure makes them particularly attractive to long-term investors seeking efficient market exposure.

Furthermore, bond ETFs offer intraday trading. Investors can buy and sell shares of a bond ETF throughout the trading day, providing greater control over their investments. This liquidity is particularly beneficial in times of market volatility or when investors need to react quickly to changing market conditions. This is a significant advantage over mutual funds, which typically only allow trades at the end of the trading day.

However, it's important to note that, like all investments, bond ETFs carry risks. Interest rate risk is a primary concern, as rising interest rates can negatively impact the value of fixed-income securities. Credit risk is another factor to consider, as the possibility of default by bond issuers can impact the performance of the ETF. Investors should carefully assess their risk tolerance and investment goals before investing in bond ETFs.

In summary, bond ETFs provide a powerful and flexible tool for investors seeking exposure to the bond market. Their liquidity, transparency, and low costs make them a compelling alternative to traditional bond mutual funds for many investors. However, it's crucial to understand the associated risks and carefully consider one's investment objectives and risk tolerance before investing.

Disclaimer: This information is for educational purposes only and is not financial advice. Consult a financial professional before making any investment decisions.

Advantages and Disadvantages of Bond ETFs

Exchange-Traded Funds (ETFs) tracking bond indexes have rapidly gained popularity among investors seeking exposure to the fixed-income market. Their structure offers several compelling advantages, but also presents certain drawbacks compared to traditional bond mutual funds. Understanding both sides of the coin is crucial for making informed investment decisions.

Advantages of Bond ETFs

- **Low Costs:** One of the most significant advantages of bond ETFs is their typically lower expense ratios compared to actively managed bond mutual funds. This translates to greater returns over the long term, as less of your investment is eaten away by fees. Passive ETFs, mirroring a bond index, naturally keep costs down.
- **Tax Efficiency:** Bond ETFs generally exhibit better tax efficiency than mutual funds. This stems from their structure; ETFs rarely distribute capital gains, while mutual funds often trigger capital gains distributions that impact your taxable income.

- **Intraday Trading:** Unlike mutual funds, which are priced only at the end of the trading day, bond ETFs trade throughout the day on exchanges. This allows for greater flexibility and the ability to react quickly to market changes. You can buy or sell shares at any point during market hours, enhancing tactical adjustments.

- **Transparency:** The holdings of a bond ETF are publicly available and updated regularly. This transparency allows investors to readily assess the underlying assets and their exposure to various sectors, maturities, and credit qualities. This facilitates informed decision-making.

- **Diversification:** Bond ETFs offer instantaneous diversification across a large number of bonds. This mitigates the risk associated with investing in individual bonds, reducing the impact of any single bond defaulting.

- **Flexibility and Control:** Investors have more control over their investment with ETFs. They can choose to buy or sell shares at any time during trading hours, unlike mutual funds where transactions are processed at the end of the day at the net asset value (NAV).

Disadvantages of Bond ETFs

- **Commission Costs:** While expense ratios are generally lower for ETFs, brokerage commissions apply each time you buy or sell shares. Frequent trading can significantly increase the overall cost of investing in bond ETFs.

- **Price Volatility:** Bond ETFs can be subject to price fluctuations throughout the trading day, unlike mutual funds priced only at the close. While this offers flexibility, it also introduces potential for losses if not managed carefully.

- **Tracking Error:** Although passively managed ETFs aim to mirror an index, a small tracking error may exist. This difference in performance stems from the difficulty in perfectly replicating a bond index, due to factors such as bid-ask spreads and transaction costs.

- **Minimum Investment:** While lower than many other investments, you still need to buy a certain number of shares to make an investment in a bond ETF. This minimum investment amount might be prohibitive for some investors with smaller capital.

- **Liquidity Risk:** While generally liquid, less popular bond ETFs might exhibit lower liquidity, making it difficult to buy or sell shares quickly without impacting the price. This is particularly true for ETFs focusing on niche bond markets.

- **Potential for Short-Term Losses:** Like other investments, bond ETFs are not immune to market downturns. Investors might experience short-term losses, especially in volatile market environments. Understanding your risk tolerance is vital.

In conclusion, bond ETFs provide several compelling advantages, such as low costs, tax efficiency, and intraday trading. However, investors should carefully consider the disadvantages, including commission costs, price volatility, and potential liquidity risks, before making investment decisions. A thorough understanding of your individual financial goals and risk tolerance is crucial to determine if bond ETFs are the right investment vehicle for you.

Comparing Bond ETFs and Bond Mutual Funds

Bond exchange-traded funds (ETFs) and bond mutual funds both offer diversified exposure to the bond market, but they differ significantly in their structure, trading mechanics, and investor implications. Understanding these differences is crucial for selecting the investment vehicle best suited to your individual financial goals and risk tolerance. This comparison will illuminate the key distinctions between these two popular investment choices.

Trading and Pricing:

One of the most significant differences lies in how they are traded. Bond mutual funds are traded directly with the fund company at the end of the trading day, based on the net asset value (NAV). This means you buy or sell shares at the calculated NAV, which reflects the closing prices of the bonds in the portfolio. In contrast, bond ETFs trade throughout the day on stock exchanges, just like individual stocks. Their price fluctuates based on supply and demand, and you can buy or sell shares at the prevailing market price, which can differ from the NAV. This intraday trading flexibility offers advantages for those seeking to time their trades or react quickly to market shifts.

Expense Ratios:

Generally, bond ETFs tend to have lower expense ratios than comparable bond mutual funds. This is primarily due to the passive nature of many ETFs, which often track an index, requiring less active management compared to actively managed mutual funds. Lower expense ratios translate directly into higher returns for investors over the long term. However, it's crucial to compare expense ratios carefully across specific funds, as some actively managed ETFs might have higher fees.

Tax Efficiency:

Both bond ETFs and mutual funds can generate capital gains distributions, impacting your tax liability. However, ETFs often exhibit greater tax efficiency than mutual funds. This is because ETFs are less likely to trigger taxable events such as frequent capital gains distributions because they rarely sell assets unless necessary for portfolio rebalancing. This tax advantage can be significant for investors holding these funds in taxable accounts.

Minimum Investment and Accessibility:

Bond ETFs typically require only a purchase of a single share, providing greater accessibility for investors with smaller capital. Mutual funds, on the other hand, may have higher minimum investment requirements, potentially excluding some investors from participating. This accessibility feature makes ETFs particularly attractive to younger investors or those just starting to build their portfolios.

Liquidity and Trading Volume:

The liquidity of a bond fund depends significantly on the volume of its trading. Bond ETFs, traded on exchanges, generally exhibit higher liquidity compared to mutual funds due to higher trading volume. This means you can usually buy or sell ETF shares more easily and quickly than mutual fund shares. This higher liquidity is particularly advantageous during market volatility when you need to quickly adjust your portfolio.

Active vs. Passive Management:

Both ETFs and mutual funds offer both actively managed and passively managed options. Actively managed funds aim to outperform the market through skillful stock picking, while passively managed funds aim to match the performance of a specific market index. While actively managed funds can potentially generate superior returns, they usually come with higher fees. Passively managed funds, on the other hand, offer a cost-effective approach. The choice between active and passive management depends largely on your investment goals and risk tolerance.

In Summary:

The choice between bond ETFs and bond mutual funds depends on individual circumstances and investment objectives. ETFs generally offer **lower costs, greater tax efficiency, and intraday trading flexibility**, making them attractive to investors who are comfortable with the nuances of exchange-traded securities. Mutual funds, on the other hand, may be more suitable for investors seeking **professional management and potentially higher returns** from actively managed strategies, albeit at a potentially higher cost. A comprehensive understanding of your investment horizon, risk profile, and tax situation is key to making an informed decision.

Trading Bond ETFs: Mechanics and Costs

Trading bond ETFs mirrors the process of trading stocks, offering a streamlined approach to accessing the bond market. However, understanding the mechanics and associated costs is crucial for maximizing returns and minimizing expenses. This section delves into the intricacies of trading bond ETFs, providing a clear picture of what to expect.

Execution: Bond ETFs trade throughout the day on major exchanges, just like stocks. You can buy and sell them through online brokerage accounts, traditional brokerage firms, or even some robo-advisors. The ease of trading is a significant advantage over individual bonds, which often involve more complex transactions and potentially higher minimum purchase amounts. Order types available for bond ETF trading typically include market orders (buying or selling at the current market price), limit orders (buying or selling only at a specified price or better), and stop-loss orders (triggering a sale when the price drops to a predetermined level). Understanding these order types is essential for managing risk and executing your trading strategy effectively. The execution speed depends on various factors, including market liquidity, the size of your trade, and your brokerage's infrastructure.

Commissions and Fees: While the low expense ratios of bond ETFs are a major draw, remember that brokerage commissions and fees apply to each trade. These fees can vary significantly among brokerages, so it pays to shop around for competitive pricing. Many brokerages offer commission-free trading for ETFs, including bond ETFs, but it's important to be aware of any other potential

30

fees, such as account maintenance fees or inactivity fees. Always carefully review your brokerage's fee schedule before initiating any trades. The cumulative effect of these fees over time, especially for frequent traders, should be factored into your overall investment analysis.

Bid-Ask Spread: Unlike stocks, bond ETFs often exhibit a wider bid-ask spread. The *bid-ask spread* is the difference between the price at which a buyer is willing to purchase (bid) and the price at which a seller is willing to sell (ask). A wider spread translates to a higher cost of trading, potentially eating into your profits. The spread is influenced by the ETF's trading volume and the underlying bond market's liquidity. Less liquid ETFs will generally have wider spreads, making them potentially less cost-effective to trade.

Slippage: Slippage refers to the difference between the expected price of a trade and the actual execution price. This can occur due to market volatility, especially during periods of heightened trading activity. **Large trades** are more susceptible to slippage, as executing a large order may move the market price. Slippage can be unpredictable, potentially impacting profitability. Careful order placement and timing can help mitigate the risk of slippage.

Tax Implications: While not directly a trading cost, the tax implications of trading bond ETFs are important to consider. Capital gains distributions from bond ETFs are subject to capital gains tax, which is dependent on your tax bracket and the holding period. Frequent trading can generate higher capital gains taxes, reducing your overall returns. A well-defined investment strategy that minimizes unnecessary trades is critical for optimizing after-tax returns.

Minimizing Costs: Several strategies can help minimize trading costs when working with bond ETFs. These include: choosing ETFs with high trading volume and liquidity to reduce bid-ask spreads; employing limit orders to ensure you only execute trades at your desired price; utilizing commission-free brokerage accounts; and adopting a long-term investment strategy to reduce the frequency of trading and associated transaction costs. By carefully considering these factors, investors can optimize their bond ETF trading experience, ensuring that costs remain low and profitability maximized.

In conclusion, while trading bond ETFs is relatively straightforward, understanding the nuances of commissions, spreads, slippage, and tax implications is essential for successful investing. By adopting informed strategies and selecting the appropriate brokerage services, investors can effectively manage costs and maximize their returns in the bond market through ETF trading.

Part II: Navigating the Bond Fund Landscape

4. Active vs. Passive Bond Management

Active Bond Fund Strategies: Sector Rotation, Yield Curve Trading, Credit Analysis

Active bond fund managers employ a range of sophisticated strategies to outperform passive benchmarks. Unlike passive funds that simply track an index, active managers actively seek opportunities to enhance returns through skillful selection and timing of bond investments. Three key strategies stand out: *sector rotation*, *yield curve trading*, and *credit analysis*. Each presents unique challenges and opportunities.

Sector Rotation involves strategically shifting allocations among different bond sectors—such as government, corporate, mortgage-backed, or high-yield—based on anticipated changes in relative performance. For instance, if an active manager anticipates a period of economic weakness, they might **increase** exposure to **high-quality government bonds** deemed safer havens, while reducing exposure to riskier corporate bonds. Conversely, during periods of economic expansion, they may favor corporate bonds or high-yield bonds to capitalize on higher potential returns. Successful sector rotation demands astute economic forecasting and an understanding of market cycles. The timing element is critical; a poorly timed shift can significantly hurt performance. Moreover, *sector rotation often involves considerable transaction costs*, which can offset gains if not managed carefully.

Yield Curve Trading leverages the relationship between bond yields and their maturities (the yield curve). The yield curve can be upward-sloping (longer-term bonds offer higher yields), downward-sloping (inverted), or flat. Active managers may **exploit anticipated shifts in the yield curve shape**. For example, if they foresee a flattening yield curve, they might **sell longer-term bonds and buy shorter-term bonds**, anticipating that the yield differential will narrow. Alternatively, if an upward-sloping yield curve is anticipated to steepen, they may **increase exposure to longer-term bonds** to benefit from the widening yield spread. This strategy necessitates accurate predictions about macroeconomic factors and interest rate movements, with miscalculations leading to significant losses.

Credit Analysis forms the bedrock of many active bond strategies, particularly within the corporate bond market. Active managers conduct rigorous assessments of individual corporate issuers' financial strength and creditworthiness before investing. They delve into company financial statements, analyze industry trends, assess management quality, and evaluate the economic environment's impact on the issuer. This deep dive allows them to identify undervalued bonds of fundamentally sound companies or to avoid bonds with high default risk that might appear superficially attractive. Effective credit analysis hinges on a strong understanding of accounting principles, financial modeling, and macroeconomic analysis. The complexity and time-intensity associated with credit analysis are significant factors, and even the most thorough credit analysis cannot fully eliminate the risk of default.

In conclusion, active bond fund managers employ a variety of sophisticated strategies to generate alpha (excess returns compared to benchmarks). Sector rotation, yield curve trading, and credit analysis all require expertise, precise timing, and a deep understanding of macroeconomic factors and market dynamics. While these strategies offer the potential for outsized returns, they also carry significant risks. <u>Investors considering active bond funds should carefully assess the manager's track record, investment philosophy, and fee structure before committing their capital.</u>

Passive Bond Fund Strategies: Index Tracking, Replication Methods

Passive bond fund management represents a stark contrast to its active counterpart. Instead of attempting to outperform the market through skillful stock picking and market timing, passive strategies aim to <u>mirror</u> the performance of a specific bond market index. This approach, rooted in the principles of modern portfolio theory, emphasizes diversification and cost efficiency. The core tenet is that consistent, long-term returns are best achieved by tracking a well-diversified benchmark rather than trying to beat it.

The most prevalent passive strategy is **index tracking**. This involves creating a portfolio that closely matches the composition and weighting of a chosen bond index, such as the Bloomberg Barclays U.S. Aggregate Bond Index or a similar international benchmark. To achieve this, the fund manager purchases bonds in proportions that reflect the index's weightings. The goal is to minimize the *tracking error* – the difference in performance between the fund and the index.

However, perfectly replicating an index is often impractical, especially for indices containing a vast number of bonds. This is where **replication methods** come into play. Several techniques exist to approximate the index's performance, each with its own strengths and weaknesses:

- **Full Replication:** This involves purchasing every single bond within the index in the exact proportions specified. This is the most accurate method but is often infeasible due to the high transaction costs and difficulties in acquiring all the bonds, particularly for less liquid bonds.

- **Stratified Sampling:** This approach divides the index into strata (e.g., based on maturity, credit rating, or sector) and then randomly samples bonds from each stratum. This approach reduces the number of bonds to be purchased while aiming to maintain a representative sample of the index's characteristics. It effectively balances accuracy and practicality.

- **Optimization:** This sophisticated technique uses mathematical algorithms to select a subset of bonds that minimizes tracking error while considering factors such as transaction costs and liquidity. This method is computationally intensive but can achieve excellent results, especially for larger indices.

- **Synthetic Replication:** This approach uses derivatives, such as swaps or futures contracts, to gain exposure to the index's returns rather than directly purchasing the underlying bonds. This method can offer cost advantages and greater flexibility, but it introduces counterparty risk – the risk that the other party in the derivative contract may default. Therefore, careful selection of counterparties is critical.

The choice of replication method depends on several factors, including the size and composition of the index, the fund's objectives, and the resources available to the fund manager. Smaller indices might be fully replicated, while larger and more diverse indices might utilize stratified sampling or optimization. Synthetic replication might be preferred when transaction costs are high or access to certain bonds is limited.

Regardless of the specific replication method, passive bond fund managers strive for *transparency and low costs*. Regular reporting on tracking error and expense ratios is essential. The emphasis is on delivering the market return, minus the minimal fees incurred in replicating the index, providing investors with a cost-effective way to gain diversified exposure to the bond market.

Ultimately, the success of a passive bond fund strategy hinges on the accurate and efficient replication of the chosen index. By minimizing tracking error and keeping costs low, passive bond funds offer investors a straightforward and often highly effective approach to bond investing.

Evaluating Active vs. Passive Management Fees and Performance

The choice between **active** and **passive** bond fund management is a crucial decision for investors, significantly impacting both *fees* and *performance*. Understanding the nuances of each approach is paramount to making an informed investment choice. This section delves into a comparative analysis of active versus passive strategies, highlighting the key factors investors should consider.

Active bond fund management involves professional fund managers who actively select individual bonds, attempting to outperform a benchmark index. These managers employ various strategies, such as **sector rotation** (shifting investments based on anticipated market movements), **yield curve trading** (exploiting differences in yields across maturities), and **credit analysis** (assessing the creditworthiness of bond issuers). The goal is to generate superior returns compared to a passive approach, but this often comes at a higher cost.

The primary driver of higher costs in active management is the **higher expense ratio**. Active fund managers require larger teams of analysts and traders, leading to increased operational expenses. These expenses are passed on to investors through higher fees, potentially eating into overall returns. Furthermore, active managers may engage in more frequent trading, incurring **transaction costs** that further reduce investor returns.

Conversely, passive bond fund management aims to replicate the performance of a specific bond index. These funds, often referred to as **index funds** or **bond ETFs**, passively track the composition and weighting of the chosen index, minimizing trading activity and consequently, reducing costs. **Index funds** typically have significantly lower expense ratios than actively managed funds, offering investors a cost-effective way to gain exposure to the bond market.

The performance implications of active versus passive management are a subject of ongoing debate. While active managers can outperform the market in certain periods, consistent outperformance over the long term is rare and difficult to predict. Many studies have shown that the majority of active bond funds fail to consistently beat their benchmark indices after adjusting for fees. The **expense ratio drag** often offsets any potential gains from superior stock-picking.

Passive strategies, on the other hand, guarantee exposure to the market at a low cost. While they may not produce spectacular returns, they consistently match the market's performance, avoiding the risk of underperformance often associated with actively managed funds. For investors seeking a cost-effective way to achieve broad bond market exposure, passive strategies often prove superior.

Ultimately, the best approach depends on individual investor preferences and goals. *Investors with a long-term horizon and a low tolerance for risk may favor passive management due to its low costs and consistent performance.* Those willing to tolerate higher fees in the pursuit of potentially higher returns, although with a higher risk of underperformance, might consider active management. However, it's *crucial to carefully analyze the historical performance, expense ratios, and risk profiles* of both active and passive bond funds before making an investment decision.

It is also important to consider the **tax implications** of both active and passive management. Active management, with its higher trading frequency, can result in higher capital gains distributions, leading to a greater tax burden for investors. Passive funds, with their lower turnover, typically generate lower capital gains distributions, resulting in potentially lower tax liabilities. Therefore, understanding the tax implications of each strategy is another critical factor in making an informed investment decision.

In conclusion, the choice between active and passive management involves a careful consideration of fees, performance potential, and risk tolerance. While active management promises potential outperformance, it comes at a higher cost and with no guarantee of success. Passive management offers a cost-effective and consistent approach, typically aligning with market returns. A thorough understanding of these factors is crucial to building a well-diversified and efficient bond portfolio.

5. Short-Term vs. Long-Term Bond Funds

Interest Rate Sensitivity and Duration

Understanding the relationship between **interest rate sensitivity** and **duration** is crucial for navigating the bond market effectively. These concepts are inextricably linked and determine how significantly a bond's price will fluctuate in response to changes in prevailing interest rates. This section delves into the intricacies of these key metrics, empowering investors to make informed decisions when constructing their bond portfolios.

Let's start with *interest rate sensitivity.* Simply put, it measures how much a bond's price changes for a given movement in interest rates. Bonds with longer maturities are generally more sensitive to interest rate fluctuations. This is because, with longer maturities, the bond's cash flows are further into the future and therefore more heavily discounted by higher interest rates. Conversely, bonds with shorter maturities show less sensitivity. A rise in interest rates will decrease the present value of a bond's future cash flows, causing its price to decline. The longer the time until those cash flows are received, the greater the price decline. The converse is also true: falling interest rates lead to an increase in bond prices, with longer-maturity bonds benefiting more. This sensitivity is not linear; the relationship is complex and influenced by numerous factors including the bond's coupon rate and the shape of the yield curve.

Now, let's examine *duration*. While interest rate sensitivity provides a qualitative understanding of price fluctuations, duration offers a more precise, quantitative measure. Duration is a weighted average of the time until each cash flow from a bond is received, weighted by the present value of that cash flow. It essentially tells us the approximate percentage change in a bond's price for a 1% change in interest rates. A bond with a duration of 5 years, for instance, would theoretically see a 5% price change for a 1% change in rates. It's important to remember that this is an approximation, as duration only provides a linear approximation of a bond's price sensitivity over small changes in interest rates.

The relationship between duration and interest rate sensitivity is direct. **Higher duration implies greater interest rate sensitivity**, and vice-versa. This relationship is a cornerstone of bond portfolio management. Investors aiming to minimize interest rate risk will favor bonds with short durations and hence lower sensitivity. Conversely, those seeking higher returns, willing to accept more risk, may consider bonds with longer durations.

Understanding duration is crucial for active bond management strategies. For example, bond managers might shorten the duration of their portfolios as interest rates are expected to rise to mitigate potential losses. Conversely, they may lengthen duration in anticipation of falling interest rates to capture the potential price appreciation. **Careful consideration of duration and interest rate sensitivity** allows for the construction of diversified bond portfolios tailored to an investor's specific risk tolerance and investment goals.

Furthermore, **duration is not just a measure for individual bonds but is also applicable to entire bond**

funds and ETFs. A fund's duration reflects the weighted average duration of the bonds it holds. Investors can use a fund's duration as a quick way to assess its overall interest rate sensitivity. This is especially helpful when comparing different funds with various underlying bond holdings.

In conclusion, a thorough grasp of interest rate sensitivity and duration is paramount for successful bond investing. By carefully analyzing these metrics, investors can make informed decisions about asset allocation, risk management, and the selection of bond funds and ETFs that align with their individual financial objectives and risk profiles. Investors should not only understand these concepts in isolation but also their interplay – recognizing that the higher a bond's duration, the greater its sensitivity to interest rate changes.

Capital Preservation vs. Growth Potential

The core tension in bond investing, and indeed in much of finance, lies in the delicate balance between capital preservation and growth potential. This dichotomy is particularly relevant when choosing between short-term and long-term bond funds, as well as when considering different bond types within a portfolio. Short-term bond funds prioritize *capital preservation*. Their shorter maturities mean that their prices are less volatile than those of longer-term bonds. This stability is particularly appealing to risk-averse investors or those with near-term financial goals. For example, someone saving for a down payment on a house within the next two years might find the relative stability of a short-term bond fund preferable to the potentially higher, but riskier, returns of a long-term fund.

Conversely, long-term bond funds generally offer greater *growth potential*. While they expose investors to more interest rate risk and price volatility, their longer maturities can yield significantly higher returns over time. This is because, in a stable interest rate environment, these longer maturities provide more opportunity for compounding returns. Investors with a longer time horizon, such as those saving for retirement decades in the future, may be more comfortable accepting this increased risk for the possibility of greater long-term growth.

The choice between capital preservation and growth potential isn't always a binary decision. Many investors seek a **balance**. For instance, a portfolio might incorporate both short-term and long-term bond funds to strategically mitigate risk while still pursuing growth. This approach allows for some capital preservation in the short term, while benefiting from the long-term growth potential of the longer-maturity holdings. The optimal balance varies according to individual risk tolerance, time horizon, and financial goals. This illustrates that a well-structured bond portfolio should be carefully crafted to achieve these individual objectives.

Furthermore, the interplay between capital preservation and growth potential is profoundly influenced by the **type of bonds** held within the fund. Investment-grade bonds, typically issued by financially stable entities, are seen as more secure and prioritize capital preservation. Their lower yields reflect the lower risk associated with this investment. On the other hand, high-yield bonds, or "junk bonds," offer a chance for higher returns, but carry a considerably higher default risk. These higher returns are a compensation for taking on increased risk. This tradeoff, too, should be carefully considered in light of the investor's specific needs and risk profile.

Moreover, *inflation* significantly impacts this crucial trade-off. During periods of high inflation, the real return (return adjusted for inflation) on bonds can diminish. The purchasing power of the principal and interest payments is reduced, making capital preservation even more challenging. Therefore, investors must consider the potential impact of inflation when striving for a balance between capital preservation and growth. Strategies like investing in inflation-protected securities (TIPS) can help address this challenge, although these may have different growth profiles compared to other bond options.

In conclusion, the decision of prioritizing capital preservation versus growth potential is a cornerstone of bond fund and ETF selection. It requires a thorough understanding of one's individual circumstances, including their risk tolerance, investment timeline, and financial aspirations. By carefully weighing the tradeoffs between these two crucial factors, investors can build a bond portfolio that effectively meets their financial goals while managing risk appropriately. A well-diversified approach, incorporating multiple fund types and strategies, is often the most effective way to navigate this complex landscape.

Optimal Asset Allocation Strategies Based on Time Horizon

Determining the ideal asset allocation, particularly the balance between bonds and other asset classes like stocks, is critically dependent on your investment time horizon. Your time horizon is simply the length of time you plan to invest your money before needing to withdraw it. A longer time horizon offers greater flexibility and risk tolerance, while a shorter horizon necessitates a more conservative approach.

For <u>long-term investors</u> (e.g., those saving for retirement decades away), a higher allocation to stocks is generally recommended. Stocks, while riskier in the short term, have historically delivered higher returns over extended periods. This approach allows for greater potential growth to offset inflation and achieve long-term financial goals. Within a long-term portfolio, bonds still play a vital role, providing diversification and reducing overall portfolio volatility. A suitable allocation might be 70% stocks and 30% bonds, though this can vary based on individual risk tolerance and other factors. The bond portion might be further diversified across different types of bond funds, such as long-term government bonds for stability and corporate bonds for potentially higher yields.

In contrast, <u>intermediate-term investors</u> (e.g., those saving for a down payment in 5-10 years) need to strike a balance between growth and capital preservation. A more balanced allocation, such as 50% stocks and 50% bonds, might be appropriate. The inclusion of short-term and intermediate-term bond funds becomes more significant here to minimize interest rate risk. These funds are less sensitive to interest rate fluctuations, providing greater stability closer to the withdrawal date. The stock portion might focus on more established, less volatile companies to limit potential losses.

For <u>short-term investors</u> (e.g., those saving for an emergency fund or a near-term purchase), a predominantly conservative allocation is essential. A portfolio heavily weighted towards bonds, perhaps 80% or more, is often recommended. Focusing on short-term bond funds and money market funds ensures principal preservation and liquidity. The risk of significant losses is greatly minimized, ensuring the funds are readily available when needed. A small allocation to stocks might still be considered, depending on individual risk tolerance, but should be minimal given the short time horizon.

Beyond Time Horizon: Other Considerations

While the time horizon is paramount, other factors also influence optimal asset allocation. These include:

- **Risk Tolerance:** Your comfort level with potential investment losses significantly impacts asset allocation. A higher risk tolerance allows for a greater allocation to stocks, while a lower tolerance suggests a more conservative approach with a higher bond allocation.
- **Financial Goals:** The specific goals you're saving for (retirement, education, down payment, etc.) will shape your asset allocation strategy. Retirement planning often involves a longer time horizon and higher stock allocation, while down payment savings may benefit from a more conservative allocation.
- **Income Needs:** If you require regular income from your investments, a higher bond allocation might be appropriate to generate steady returns, though you might consider dividend-paying stocks as well.
- **Tax Implications:** Tax-advantaged accounts (such as 401(k)s and IRAs) can influence asset allocation decisions, allowing for a potentially greater allocation to higher-yielding tax-inefficient investments, such as municipal bonds.

Professional Guidance:

It's important to remember that asset allocation is a personalized process. Seeking advice from a qualified financial advisor can provide valuable insights tailored to your specific circumstances, risk tolerance, and financial goals. They can help you develop a comprehensive investment strategy that aligns with your time horizon and overall financial objectives, ensuring you're on the right track towards achieving your financial aspirations.

6. High-Yield vs. Investment-Grade Bond Funds

Risk and Reward Trade-off

The fundamental principle governing investment decisions, particularly within the realm of **high-yield** and **investment-grade bond funds**, is the inextricable link between risk and reward. This concept dictates that higher potential returns are invariably accompanied by a greater degree of risk, and conversely, lower risk investments generally offer more modest returns. Understanding this trade-off is paramount to making informed investment choices aligned with individual risk tolerance and financial objectives.

High-yield bond funds, often referred to as "junk bonds," represent a segment of the fixed-income market characterized by higher yields but also significantly elevated default risk. These bonds are issued by companies with lower credit ratings, implying a higher probability of default or failure to meet their debt obligations. While the allure of potentially higher returns is undeniable, investors must carefully weigh this against the very real possibility of substantial capital losses. The potential reward – a higher yield than investment-grade bonds – is directly tied to the increased risk of default.

In contrast, **investment-grade bond funds** are considered relatively safer investments, offering lower yields but a reduced likelihood of default. These bonds are issued by companies and governments with strong credit ratings, indicating a greater capacity to meet their payment obligations. The lower risk associated with investment-grade bonds translates to lower yields, making them a more conservative choice suitable for risk-averse investors prioritizing capital preservation over aggressive growth. The reward here is stability and reduced risk of principal loss, making them ideal for individuals with lower risk tolerance or those approaching retirement.

The **risk-reward spectrum** is not a binary choice but rather a continuum. Different bond funds occupy various points along this spectrum, offering a range of risk-return profiles to suit diverse investor needs. For example, some funds might strategically blend high-yield and investment-grade bonds to achieve a balance between risk and reward, seeking to maximize returns while mitigating overall portfolio volatility. This approach requires a sophisticated understanding of market dynamics and careful consideration of the fund's investment strategy.

A crucial aspect of assessing this trade-off involves understanding the **credit ratings** assigned to the bonds within a particular fund. Agencies like Moody's, Standard & Poor's, and Fitch provide independent credit assessments, offering investors valuable insights into the creditworthiness of bond issuers. Higher credit ratings (AAA, AA, A) indicate lower default risk and typically correlate with lower yields, whereas lower ratings (BB, B, CCC) suggest higher default risk and correspondingly higher yields. Investors should meticulously examine these ratings to gauge the level of risk inherent in a specific fund.

Beyond credit ratings, other factors contribute to the risk-reward equation. **Interest rate risk**, for instance, affects the value of bonds inversely; rising interest rates typically lead to lower bond prices, and vice versa. **Inflation risk** also plays a role, as inflation can erode the real return of fixed-income investments. A comprehensive risk assessment must account for these factors, alongside others like **reinvestment risk** and **liquidity risk**.

Ultimately, the optimal risk-reward trade-off is subjective and depends heavily on an individual's financial goals, time horizon, and risk tolerance. Aggressive investors with a longer time horizon may favor higher-yield funds, accepting greater risk for the potential of higher returns. Conversely, more conservative investors with a shorter time horizon may prefer investment-grade funds, prioritizing capital preservation over aggressive growth. Thorough due diligence, a clear understanding of risk, and alignment with personal investment objectives are indispensable for navigating the complexities of this crucial trade-off.

Credit Ratings and Default Risk

Understanding credit ratings and default risk is paramount when investing in bond funds, particularly those holding high-yield or non-investment grade bonds. Credit rating agencies, such as Moody's, Standard & Poor's, and Fitch, assess the creditworthiness of bond issuers, providing investors with an independent evaluation of the likelihood of default. These ratings, typically ranging from AAA (highest quality) to D (default), offer a crucial signal of the risk level associated with a particular bond.

Investment-grade bonds generally carry ratings of BBB- or higher (depending on the agency), indicating a relatively lower probability of default. Investors seeking *capital preservation* and *predictable income* often favor these bonds. However, the returns from investment-grade bonds are typically more moderate compared to higher-risk alternatives.

Conversely, **high-yield bonds**, also known as **junk bonds**, hold ratings below BBB-. These bonds offer the potential for **higher yields** to compensate for the significantly **increased risk of default**. Investing in high-yield bonds can significantly enhance potential returns but also entails the possibility of substantial principal loss if the issuer fails to meet its obligations. The default risk associated with these bonds necessitates a thorough understanding of the issuer's financial health and the overall economic environment.

The *impact of default* can vary depending on the structure of the bond fund. In actively managed funds, managers might actively mitigate default risk through careful credit analysis and diversification. However, even diversified portfolios are not immune to losses from defaults. The level of default risk exposure often directly correlates with the fund's stated investment objective, risk tolerance, and associated yield profile. Passive funds that track a specific bond index will reflect the default rates inherent within that index. Consequently, investors in such funds may experience capital losses if the underlying index suffers defaults within its constituent bonds.

Furthermore, **credit ratings are not foolproof**. While they offer valuable guidance, they are not a guarantee against default. Rating agencies' assessments can be subject to error or revisions based on new information. Economic downturns, unexpected industry disruptions, or issuer-specific events can all influence the likelihood of default. Hence, thorough due diligence is crucial before investing in any bond fund, irrespective of its credit rating.

Understanding the specific risks associated with the fund's holdings, as detailed in the prospectus, enables more informed investment decisions.

Therefore, investors should carefully **consider their risk tolerance** and **investment goals** when choosing between high-yield and investment-grade bond funds. While high-yield bonds might offer tempting yields, the **potential for losses** requires careful consideration and a more thorough analysis of the issuers' financial health. A balanced approach that carefully assesses risk alongside potential reward is essential for building a successful bond portfolio.

Disclaimer: This information is for educational purposes only and should not be considered investment advice. Consulting with a qualified financial advisor before making any investment decisions is highly recommended.

Suitable Investor Profiles for High-Yield vs. Investment-Grade Bond Funds

The decision between investing in high-yield (**high-risk, high-reward**) or investment-grade (**lower-risk, lower-reward**) bond funds hinges significantly on the investor's unique *risk tolerance*, *financial goals*, and *time horizon*. Understanding these factors is crucial for making an informed investment choice that aligns with individual circumstances.

High-Yield Bond Funds: A Profile of Suitable Investors

- **Aggressive Investors with Long Time Horizons:** High-yield funds, often referred to as "junk bonds," carry substantial default risk. Investors comfortable with the possibility of principal loss and willing to accept higher volatility over an extended period (e.g., 10 years or more) might find them suitable. This strategy prioritizes potential for higher returns to outpace inflation and achieve significant long-term growth.

- **Investors with High Risk Tolerance and Diversified Portfolios:** High-yield bond exposure should not represent a significant portion of a portfolio, particularly for those with lower risk tolerance. Diversification across asset classes (stocks, real estate, etc.) is essential to mitigate the risk associated with high-yield bonds. Their inclusion should be carefully considered as a way to enhance returns within a well-diversified strategy, not as the core of the investment plan.

- **Sophisticated Investors with Understanding of Credit Risk:** Evaluating the creditworthiness of individual issuers is essential. Investors should possess a strong grasp of financial statements, credit ratings (Moody's, S&P, Fitch), and the factors influencing default risk. Independent research and analysis are paramount before allocating to high-yield funds.

- **Investors Seeking Higher Income Potential:** High-yield bonds offer the potential for significantly higher yields compared to investment-grade bonds. Investors prioritizing current income generation, such as retirees needing a stable income stream, might consider a modest allocation if their risk tolerance permits. However, it's crucial to balance income needs against the risk of capital losses.

Investment-Grade Bond Funds: A Profile of Suitable Investors

- **Conservative Investors with Low Risk Tolerance:** Investment-grade bonds are characterized by their lower risk of default. Investors prioritizing capital preservation and stability over maximizing returns will find investment-grade funds more appealing. This profile often involves individuals with shorter time horizons or those nearing retirement who want to minimize the chance of significant losses.

- **Investors Seeking Predictable Income Streams:** Investment-grade bonds offer more stable and predictable income streams compared to high-yield bonds. This is attractive to investors seeking regular dividend payments, such as retirees relying on fixed income for living expenses. The focus is on consistency and reliability of income rather than aggressive growth.

- **Investors with Shorter Time Horizons:** The lower risk associated with investment-grade bonds makes them suitable for those needing access to their funds in the near future (e.g., within 5 years). The lower volatility and stability limit potential losses closer to maturity.

- **Risk-Averse Investors Seeking Diversification:** Investment-grade bonds serve as an important diversifier within a broader portfolio. Their lower correlation with stocks can reduce overall portfolio volatility. Many investors value this stability as a counterbalance to higher-risk asset classes, thereby reducing the portfolio's overall sensitivity to market fluctuations.

Disclaimer: This information is for educational purposes only and does not constitute financial advice. Investors should conduct thorough research and consult with a qualified financial advisor before making any investment decisions. Individual circumstances and financial goals vary greatly, necessitating personalized advice tailored to each investor's unique profile.

7. Municipal Bond Funds: Tax Advantages and Considerations

Types of Municipal Bonds: General Obligation, Revenue

Municipal bonds, often called *munis*, are debt securities issued by state and local governments to finance public projects. They offer a compelling combination of *tax advantages* and *relatively low risk*, making them a staple in many diversified portfolios. However, understanding the nuances of different muni types is crucial for informed investment decisions. Two primary categories dominate the municipal bond landscape: **general obligation bonds** and **revenue bonds**.

General Obligation Bonds (GO Bonds): These bonds are backed by the **full faith and credit** of the issuing municipality. This means repayment relies on the municipality's **overall taxing power** to raise funds for debt service. If the municipality struggles to meet its obligations, it can increase property taxes, sales taxes, or other forms of taxation to make the necessary payments. This backing makes GO bonds generally considered **lower risk** than revenue bonds, albeit with potentially lower yields. The creditworthiness of the issuing municipality, typically rated by credit agencies like Moody's, S&P, and Fitch, is paramount in assessing the risk profile of GO bonds.

Examples of projects financed through GO bonds include schools, hospitals, public works infrastructure (roads, bridges, water systems), and other essential public services. Investors should carefully analyze the issuer's financial health, including factors like its debt levels, tax base, and overall economic conditions, to understand the potential risks associated with GO bonds. **Higher-rated GO bonds** from financially stable municipalities offer greater security, while bonds from municipalities with weaker financial positions may carry higher yields to compensate for increased default risk.

Revenue Bonds: Unlike GO bonds, revenue bonds are secured by the **revenue generated by a specific project** they finance. For instance, revenue bonds might be issued to fund the construction of a toll road, a new airport terminal, or a water treatment plant. Repayment of these bonds depends entirely on the **ability of the project to generate sufficient revenue** to cover debt service. This makes them inherently **riskier** than GO bonds, as project revenue can fluctuate due to economic conditions, changing demand, or unforeseen operational issues. Consequently, revenue bonds usually offer **higher yields** to attract investors willing to accept this greater risk.

The analysis of revenue bonds requires a thorough examination of the project's feasibility and projected revenue streams. Factors like user fees, operating expenses, and potential competition all impact the bond's creditworthiness. While revenue bonds can offer attractive returns, they are generally *not suitable* for investors with a low risk tolerance. A detailed review of the project's financial projections, operating history (if applicable), and management capabilities is essential before investing in revenue bonds.

In summary, **GO bonds** offer a lower-risk, although potentially lower-return, investment backed by the taxing power of the issuer, while **revenue bonds** offer higher-risk, higher-return opportunities backed by the revenue generated by a specific project. Careful consideration of risk tolerance and investment goals is vital when choosing between these two major types of municipal bonds. Furthermore, *professional financial advice* is strongly recommended before making any investment decisions in municipal bonds, or any other investment security.

Tax Implications for Different Investor Brackets

Understanding the tax implications of municipal bond funds is crucial for investors, as these implications vary significantly depending on the investor's tax bracket. The primary advantage of municipal bonds, and thus municipal bond funds, is their tax-exempt status on the federal level. This means that the interest income earned from these bonds is not subject to federal income tax. However, the tax benefits are not uniform across all investors.

For **high-income earners**, the tax-exempt nature of municipal bonds becomes particularly attractive. Because they face higher marginal tax rates, the savings from avoiding federal income tax on interest income are considerably greater. The effective yield, which takes into account the tax benefits, is substantially higher for high-income individuals compared to those in lower tax brackets. In essence, the after-tax return surpasses the pre-tax return by a significant margin for this demographic. This makes municipal bond funds a compelling investment choice for high-income individuals seeking to maximize their after-tax returns.

Conversely, **investors in lower tax brackets** may not realize the same level of tax advantage. Their lower marginal tax rates mean the tax savings from the exemption are proportionally less significant. The effective yield enhancement might be less substantial, potentially leading them to consider other investment options offering higher pre-tax returns. While still offering a tax benefit, it might be less impactful in their overall financial picture than it would be for a higher-income investor. A careful evaluation of the relative benefits, including the potential for capital appreciation, is needed for this group.

Furthermore, the tax situation becomes more complex when considering state and local taxes. While interest income from municipal bonds is generally exempt from *federal* income tax, it may still be subject to *state and local taxes*, depending on the issuer. Bonds issued by a municipality within the investor's state of residence are typically exempt from state and local taxes. However, bonds from other states could be subject to taxation at the state and local levels, offsetting some of the federal tax advantages. Investors should carefully examine the specific tax characteristics of each bond within the fund to accurately assess their personal tax liability.

The **complexity increases** further for investors in multiple tax jurisdictions or those with significant other sources of income. Tax planning strategies might need to be integrated with the overall investment plan. Professional financial advice should be sought in such situations to ensure optimal tax efficiency. Sophisticated investors may use municipal bonds strategically within their portfolios to minimize their overall tax burden, potentially involving techniques like tax-loss harvesting and other advanced tax-minimization methods.

In conclusion, the tax implications of investing in municipal bond funds are not one-size-fits-all. The tax benefits are highly dependent on the investor's marginal tax rate, the issuer's location, and the investor's overall financial situation. *Understanding these nuances is paramount for making informed investment decisions.* Investors should consult with tax professionals to fully grasp the tax consequences and ensure the investment aligns with their personal tax planning objectives. Failing to do so could lead to unexpected tax liabilities and reduce the overall effectiveness of the investment strategy.

Creditworthiness of Municipal Issuers

Assessing the creditworthiness of municipal issuers is crucial for investors considering municipal bond funds. Unlike corporate bonds backed by a company's assets, municipal bonds are backed by the taxing power or revenue-generating capacity of the issuing municipality (city, county, state, or other local government entity). This introduces a unique layer of complexity to credit analysis.

Several key factors influence a municipal issuer's credit rating, which directly impacts the bond's yield and risk. **Rating agencies**, such as Moody's, Standard & Poor's, and Fitch, meticulously evaluate these factors. A higher rating signifies lower risk and, consequently, a lower yield, while a lower rating indicates higher risk and a higher yield to compensate for the increased probability of default.

Among the most important factors considered are:

- *Financial strength:* This involves analyzing the municipality's budget, revenue streams (property taxes, sales taxes, fees), and expenditure patterns. A healthy budget with sufficient reserves to cover unexpected events and debt obligations is a positive indicator.

- *Debt burden:* The level of existing debt relative to the municipality's revenue is a key measure. High debt levels can strain the municipality's ability to meet its obligations, increasing the risk of default. This includes evaluating the maturity schedule of existing debt, identifying any significant upcoming debt repayments.

- *Economic conditions:* The underlying economic health of the municipality plays a significant role. Strong economic growth, a diverse tax base, and low unemployment rates contribute to a municipality's ability to meet its debt obligations. Conversely, economic downturns can severely impact tax revenues and increase the risk of default.

- *Management and governance:* The quality of the municipality's financial management and governance structure is crucial. Competent financial management, transparent budgeting practices, and effective oversight minimize the risk of mismanagement and financial irregularities.

- *Legal and regulatory framework:* The legal and regulatory environment governing the municipality's debt issuance and management also matters. Clear legal frameworks, robust debt management procedures, and adherence to regulations enhance creditworthiness.

- *Specific project risk (for revenue bonds):* Revenue bonds are secured by the revenue generated from a specific project (e.g., toll road, water treatment plant). Credit analysis for revenue bonds requires a thorough assessment of the project's feasibility, projected revenue streams, and the management's ability to operate and maintain the project efficiently. Factors such as competition, changing market conditions, and technological obsolescence need to be considered.

Investors should carefully review the credit ratings assigned to municipal bonds by reputable rating agencies. They should also conduct **independent research** to gain a comprehensive understanding of the issuer's financial health and the associated risks. Diversification across different municipal issuers and careful monitoring of credit ratings are essential to mitigate the risks inherent in investing in municipal bonds.

Understanding the intricacies of municipal issuer creditworthiness is paramount for successful investing in municipal bond funds. A thorough and nuanced analysis of the factors outlined above allows investors to make informed decisions, balancing risk and return effectively.

8. Government Bond Funds: Stability and Security

Treasury Bonds, Notes, and Bills

The U.S. Treasury Department issues a range of debt securities, collectively known as **Treasury securities**, to finance government operations. These securities are considered among the *safest investments* globally due to the backing of the full faith and credit of the U.S. government. They are a cornerstone of many investment portfolios, offering a balance between stability and income generation. Understanding their differences is key to effective portfolio construction.

Treasury Bills (T-Bills) are short-term debt instruments maturing in **one year or less**. They are sold at a **discount** to their face value and do not pay periodic interest. Investors receive the face value at maturity, representing their return. The shorter maturity minimizes interest rate risk, making them attractive for investors seeking short-term liquidity and relative safety. T-Bills are auctioned regularly by the Treasury, providing ample opportunity for participation. Their simplicity and low risk make them a preferred choice for conservative investors.

Treasury Notes (T-Notes) are intermediate-term securities with maturities ranging **from two to ten years**. Unlike T-Bills, T-Notes pay **interest** semi-annually until maturity. This interest is calculated based on the security's face value and coupon rate. The coupon rate is set at auction, and the semi-annual payments provide a steady income stream. Investors may also benefit from potential *capital appreciation* if interest rates decline after the purchase. T-Notes offer a balance between risk and return, appealing to investors with moderate risk tolerance.

Treasury Bonds (T-Bonds) are long-term securities with maturities of **more than ten years**, often extending to 30 years. Similar to T-Notes, T-Bonds pay interest **semi-annually** until maturity. Their longer maturity results in **greater interest rate risk** compared to T-Notes and T-Bills; however, this also translates into the **potential for higher returns** over their lifetime. T-Bonds are an attractive option for investors seeking long-term, fixed-income investments, often as part of a retirement strategy or a long-term savings plan. However, their susceptibility to interest rate fluctuations warrants careful consideration.

The **risk-return profile** of Treasury Bills, Notes, and Bonds varies significantly based on their maturity. T-Bills represent the least risky option with the lowest potential return, while T-Bonds carry the highest interest rate risk but offer the potential for higher returns over the long term. The choice among these securities depends greatly on an investor's **individual risk tolerance, investment horizon, and financial goals**. A diversified approach incorporating various maturities often proves to be the most effective strategy.

Beyond the fundamental differences in maturity, it's crucial for investors to understand the nuances of *Treasury Inflation-Protected Securities (TIPS)*. These bonds adjust their principal based on the Consumer Price Index (CPI), providing a hedge against inflation. TIPS offer a unique combination of safety and inflation protection, attracting investors concerned about the erosion of purchasing power. The choice between regular Treasury securities and TIPS depends on the investor's inflation outlook and risk preferences.

Agency Bonds: GNMA, FNMA, FHLMC

Agency bonds represent a unique segment within the fixed-income market, offering investors a blend of stability and yield often exceeding that of traditional Treasury securities. These bonds are issued by **government-sponsored enterprises (GSEs)**, entities created by the US government to enhance access to credit in specific sectors, primarily housing. While not explicitly backed by the full faith and credit of the US Treasury, they enjoy an implicit government guarantee, resulting in a lower perceived risk compared to corporate bonds of similar maturity.

Let's delve into the three major players: **GNMA (Government National Mortgage Association), FNMA (Federal National Mortgage Association), and FHLMC (Federal Home Loan Mortgage Corporation)**. Understanding their distinct roles and the nature of the securities they issue is crucial for investors navigating the agency bond market.

GNMA (Ginnie Mae): The Government's Direct Involvement

Unlike Fannie Mae and Freddie Mac, *GNMA* is a wholly-owned government corporation. This direct governmental backing offers investors the highest level of security among agency bonds. Ginnie Mae does not issue bonds itself; instead, it guarantees mortgage-backed securities (MBS) issued by private lenders. These MBS pool together numerous mortgages, offering investors a diversified stream of payments backed by the underlying home loans. The government guarantee ensures timely principal and interest payments, even if the underlying mortgages default. This makes Ginnie Mae MBS particularly attractive to investors seeking *high levels of safety* and predictable income streams.

FNMA (Fannie Mae): A Private Company with Implicit Government Backing

Fannie Mae is a ***privately-owned, publicly-traded company*** that purchases mortgages from lenders, pools them into MBS, and sells these securities to investors. While not directly backed by the US government, Fannie Mae benefited from an implicit government guarantee for many years, ensuring it could access capital at favorable rates. Following the 2008 financial crisis, the government intervened extensively, ultimately placing Fannie Mae into conservatorship. The implicit government support has been maintained, albeit with ongoing government oversight and capital requirements. This creates a situation where the risk is mitigated yet not fully eliminated compared to GNMA. Fannie Mae's MBS provide a balance of *yield and relatively low risk*.

FHLMC (Freddie Mac): Similar to Fannie Mae, but Focused on Savings Institutions

Freddie Mac, similar to Fannie Mae, is a ***privately-owned, publicly-traded company*** that operates in the secondary mortgage market. However, Freddie Mac's primary focus was (and continues to be) purchasing mortgages from savings and loan associations and other thrift institutions. Like Fannie Mae, Freddie Mac pools these mortgages into MBS and sells them to investors. It also operates under a framework of implicit government backing, providing investors with similar risk profiles to Fannie Mae securities. The government's role in supporting these enterprises emphasizes that the perceived risk is considerably reduced compared to corporate bonds with the same maturity, presenting a *moderate risk, moderate return* investment opportunity.

Investing in Agency MBS: Key Considerations

Investing in agency bonds, particularly through bond funds or ETFs, offers diversification and income generation. However, several factors require careful consideration:

- **Interest Rate Risk:** Like all fixed-income securities, agency MBS are subject to interest rate risk. Rising interest rates will generally decrease the value of these bonds.

- **Prepayment Risk:** Homeowners may refinance or pay off their mortgages earlier than anticipated, impacting the cash flow from agency MBS. This prepayment risk can be more pronounced during periods of falling interest rates.

- **Credit Risk (Though Low):** While agency MBS have implicit government support, credit risk is not entirely eliminated. The risk is significantly lower compared to corporate bonds, but not entirely absent. Understanding the guarantor's financial health is still crucial.

- **Inflation Risk:** The real return on agency MBS can be eroded by inflation. Investors should consider TIPS (Treasury Inflation-Protected Securities) as a hedge against this risk.

By understanding the distinctions between GNMA, FNMA, and FHLMC and carefully evaluating the associated risks, investors can make informed decisions when incorporating agency bonds into their portfolios, benefiting from their combination of **stability and income potential**.

Inflation-Protected Securities (TIPS)

Treasury Inflation-Protected Securities, or TIPS, offer a unique and compelling solution for investors seeking to mitigate the erosion of purchasing power caused by inflation. Unlike traditional bonds, whose fixed payments are vulnerable to inflation's relentless creep, TIPS adjust their principal value based on changes in the Consumer Price Index (CPI). This principal adjustment directly impacts the semiannual interest payments, ensuring that the investor's returns keep pace with inflation, at least to the extent the CPI accurately reflects true inflation. This inherent inflation protection makes TIPS a crucial component of a well-diversified portfolio, particularly for investors with a long-term horizon and a significant concern about inflation's potential impact on their savings.

The mechanics of TIPS are straightforward yet powerfully effective. When you purchase a TIPS bond, you acquire a security with a fixed real interest rate. This real rate represents the return you will receive *above* the rate of inflation. The actual interest payments, however, are calculated based on the adjusted principal, which fluctuates with the CPI. For example, if the CPI increases, the principal value of your TIPS bond increases proportionally, leading to higher interest payments. Conversely, if inflation slows or even falls, the principal adjusts downward, reflecting the reduced impact of inflation. However, it's important to remember that the principal can never fall below its original face value at issuance.

The <u>advantage</u> of TIPS is their ability to protect against inflation risk, a risk that often plagues traditional fixed-income investments. This makes them particularly attractive during periods of high or rising inflation, offering a degree of certainty and stability that other bond types cannot match. This inherent protection is particularly beneficial for long-term investors who are concerned about the gradual erosion of their purchasing power over time. Because of this protective nature, TIPS can be a valuable tool for retirement planning, ensuring that retirement income retains its value throughout retirement years. Moreover, TIPS often provide a superior return relative to traditional bonds during inflationary periods because their yield remains attractive and their principal increases along with inflation. The real yield stays constant throughout the life of the bond, unlike a typical bond whose yield becomes less attractive as inflation rises.

However, it is important to note that TIPS are not without their drawbacks. Although they are a hedge against inflation, they might underperform traditional bonds during periods of *low* or *deflationary* environments. The real interest rate on TIPS might appear lower than yields on other types of bonds when inflation is subdued, making them less attractive in a low-inflation economy. Also, like all bonds, TIPS carry interest rate risk. Changes in overall interest rates in the broader economy can impact their market prices and affect their performance. Therefore, investors should have a solid understanding of their overall financial goals and the risks involved before including TIPS in their portfolio.

Investing in TIPS can be done directly through the U.S. Treasury Department's TreasuryDirect website, or indirectly via bond mutual funds or ETFs that specialize in TIPS. These investment vehicles offer investors access to TIPS with varying maturities and risk profiles, enabling diversified exposure to inflation-protected securities without the need to purchase and manage individual bonds directly. Investors should carefully consider the expense ratios and investment strategies of these funds to select those that align with their personal financial goals and risk tolerance.

In conclusion, Treasury Inflation-Protected Securities (TIPS) represent a valuable tool for investors seeking to safeguard their portfolios against the corrosive effects of inflation. Their unique structure, which automatically adjusts the principal based on changes in the CPI, provides an effective hedge against inflation risk, making them a worthy consideration for inclusion within a well-diversified investment strategy. However, investors should carefully weigh the potential benefits against the risks associated with their use, such as underperformance during deflationary periods and the inherent interest rate risk that applies to all bonds.

9. Corporate Bond Funds: Diversification and Sector Exposure

Different Corporate Bond Sectors: Industrials, Financials, Utilities

The corporate bond market offers a diverse landscape of investment opportunities, categorized broadly into industrials, financials, and utilities. Each sector presents a unique risk-return profile, influenced by factors specific to its underlying businesses and the broader economic environment. Understanding these distinctions is crucial for constructing a well-diversified bond portfolio.

Industrials encompass a vast array of companies involved in manufacturing, production, and distribution of goods. This sector is inherently cyclical, meaning its performance tends to mirror the overall health of the economy. During periods of economic expansion, industrial companies often experience increased demand and profitability, leading to stronger bond performance. Conversely, economic downturns can significantly impact their creditworthiness, potentially increasing default risk. Examples include automotive manufacturers, technology firms, and consumer goods companies. Investing in industrial bonds can offer attractive yields but demands careful consideration of economic cycles and the specific financial health of the issuing company.

The **Financials** sector comprises banks, insurance companies, investment firms, and other financial institutions. This sector is characterized by its sensitivity to interest rate changes and regulatory environment. Rising interest rates can squeeze profitability, while stringent regulations can impact lending practices and profitability. Conversely, a robust economic environment often boosts lending activity and financial performance. *Investing in financial bonds* requires close monitoring of interest rate trends, regulatory changes, and the overall stability of the financial system. Careful credit analysis is essential due to the interconnected nature of financial institutions.

Utilities represent a more defensive sector, encompassing companies providing essential services such as electricity, gas, water, and telecommunications. These businesses tend to exhibit greater stability due to the consistent demand for their services. Utility bonds often offer lower yields compared to industrial or financial bonds, reflecting their lower risk profile. However, their stable earnings and predictable cash flows can be particularly appealing to investors seeking income and relative stability in their portfolios. Regulatory changes, environmental concerns, and competition can still affect the performance of utility companies, necessitating due diligence.

Diversification across these sectors is a key strategy in corporate bond investing. Allocating capital across industrials, financials, and utilities can help mitigate risk by reducing exposure to sector-specific downturns. A balanced approach, tailored to an investor's risk tolerance and financial goals, is essential for maximizing returns while minimizing potential losses. It's important to remember that credit quality, maturity, and coupon rates should also be considered within each sector to achieve optimal portfolio diversification and yield.

In conclusion, understanding the distinct characteristics of industrial, financial, and utility corporate bond sectors is vital for making informed investment decisions. Each sector presents a unique risk-reward proposition, and a well-informed strategy involves carefully weighing these factors to create a portfolio that aligns with your individual financial objectives.

Analyzing Corporate Creditworthiness

Investing in corporate bonds involves inherent risk, and understanding a corporation's creditworthiness is paramount to mitigating potential losses. This section delves into the crucial aspects of assessing the credit risk associated with corporate bond issuers, enabling investors to make informed decisions within the complex landscape of corporate debt.

The cornerstone of analyzing corporate creditworthiness lies in a thorough evaluation of a company's financial health. This involves a meticulous examination of several key financial ratios and metrics. Key ratios such as the *debt-to-equity ratio*, which indicates the proportion of a company's financing from debt versus equity, provides insights into its financial leverage. A high debt-to-equity ratio might signal increased financial risk, as a heavily indebted company may struggle to meet its obligations during economic downturns. Conversely, a low debt-to-equity ratio suggests a more conservative financial structure and reduced risk.

Another crucial metric is the *interest coverage ratio*, which measures a company's ability to meet its interest payments. This ratio, calculated by dividing earnings before interest and taxes (EBIT) by interest expense, provides a critical indicator of a company's ability to service its debt obligations. A low interest coverage ratio indicates a higher probability of default, as the company might struggle to cover its interest expenses, whereas a high ratio suggests greater financial strength and stability.

Beyond basic financial ratios, creditworthiness assessments incorporate qualitative factors such as management quality, business model sustainability, and industry outlook. A company with a strong and experienced management team, a resilient business model adaptable to changing market conditions, and operating within a robust industry sector is likely to demonstrate higher creditworthiness. Conversely, companies operating in declining industries, plagued by poor management practices, or facing significant competitive pressures might carry higher levels of credit risk.

     The use of **credit ratings** provided by reputable agencies such as Moody's, Standard & Poor's, and Fitch is essential in assessing corporate creditworthiness. These agencies assign letter ratings that reflect the probability of default. Higher ratings (e.g., AAA, AA) signify lower default risk, while lower ratings (e.g., BB, B, CCC) indicate significantly higher risk. It's crucial to understand that these ratings are not infallible and should be considered alongside other factors.

Furthermore, evaluating a corporation's cash flow is critical. While profitability is significant, it doesn't always translate directly into cash readily available to meet debt obligations. A company might be profitable on paper but still lack sufficient liquid assets to service its debt. Analyzing operating cash flow and free cash flow provides a more comprehensive understanding of a company's ability to generate funds for debt repayment.

Finally, understanding the *terms and covenants of the bond indenture* itself is crucial. The bond indenture outlines the terms and conditions of the loan, including payment schedules, collateral, and protective covenants. Analyzing these terms helps understand the level of protection afforded to bondholders in case of default. Protective covenants might include restrictions on additional borrowing, dividend payments, or asset sales designed to improve the safety of the debt investment.

In conclusion, analyzing corporate creditworthiness necessitates a multi-faceted approach. It's not simply about crunching numbers; it's about developing a holistic understanding of the company's financial health, management quality, industry dynamics, and the specific terms of the bond issuance. By integrating quantitative and qualitative factors, investors can significantly enhance their ability to select corporate bonds that align with their risk tolerance and investment objectives.

Impact of Economic Cycles

Economic cycles, characterized by periods of expansion and contraction, exert a significant influence on the performance of corporate bond funds. Understanding this interplay is crucial for investors seeking to navigate the complexities of the bond market. During economic expansions, businesses generally thrive, leading to increased profitability and a lower risk of default. This positive environment translates into higher demand for corporate bonds, driving up their prices and pushing yields down. Investors in corporate bond funds benefit from capital appreciation during these periods, although the return on investment might be relatively modest due to lower yields. The stability and predictability of corporate earnings during expansions make them particularly attractive for conservative investors seeking income generation.

Conversely, economic contractions or recessions present a different picture. As businesses struggle with declining sales and profitability, the risk of default on corporate bonds increases. This heightened risk causes investors to demand higher yields as compensation, leading to a decline in bond prices. Corporate bond funds can experience significant losses during recessions, particularly those heavily invested in lower-rated bonds. The volatility of corporate bond prices during economic downturns can be substantial, impacting both income and capital appreciation. Investors need to be prepared for potential losses and carefully consider their risk tolerance before investing in corporate bond funds during uncertain economic times.

The duration of the bond also plays a significant role in how it reacts to economic cycles. Longer-duration bonds, which have longer maturities, are more sensitive to changes in interest rates. During economic expansions, the central bank may raise interest rates to curb inflation, leading to a decline in the value of longer-duration bonds. Conversely, during recessions, interest rates may be lowered to stimulate economic growth, benefiting longer-duration bonds. Shorter-duration bonds, on the other hand, are less sensitive to interest rate changes and tend to be more stable during economic fluctuations.

Furthermore, the specific sector composition of a corporate bond fund significantly influences its performance during economic cycles. Certain sectors, such as consumer discretionary or technology, tend to be more cyclical and sensitive to economic downturns. Funds with heavy exposure to these sectors may experience greater volatility during recessions. Conversely, more defensive sectors, such as utilities or healthcare, tend to be less cyclical and provide greater stability during economic contractions. Investors should carefully analyze the sector allocation of a corporate bond fund to assess its resilience to economic fluctuations.

Therefore, diversification across various sectors is paramount for mitigating risk.

Moreover, the credit quality of the bonds held within the fund is a critical factor. Investment-grade bonds, rated higher by credit rating agencies, tend to perform better during economic downturns compared to high-yield or speculative-grade bonds. However, even investment-grade bonds are not immune to the effects of economic cycles. Their prices may still decline during recessions, though generally to a lesser extent than high-yield bonds. Investors seeking higher yields should carefully weigh the increased risk associated with high-yield bonds during economic uncertainties.

In summary, economic cycles significantly impact the performance of corporate bond funds. Understanding the relationship between economic phases and bond prices, duration, sector composition, and credit quality is crucial for making informed investment decisions. Investors should adopt a well-diversified approach, considering various factors such as risk tolerance, investment time horizon, and the prevailing economic climate, to navigate the complexities of the bond market effectively and potentially mitigate the negative effects of economic downturns.

10. International Bond Funds: Global Diversification

Currency Risk and Hedging Strategies

Investing in **international bond funds** exposes investors to *currency risk*, the fluctuation in the value of a foreign currency relative to the investor's domestic currency. This risk can significantly impact returns, both positively and negatively. A strengthening domestic currency will diminish the value of foreign bond returns when converted back to the home currency, while a weakening domestic currency will enhance them. Effectively managing this risk is crucial for successful international bond investing.

One of the primary methods for mitigating currency risk is **hedging**. *Hedging strategies* aim to neutralize the impact of currency fluctuations. These strategies typically involve using financial instruments, such as **currency forwards, futures, or options**, to offset potential losses from currency movements. For example, an investor holding a bond denominated in Euros could enter into a currency forward contract to sell Euros at a predetermined exchange rate in the future, effectively locking in the exchange rate and eliminating the uncertainty associated with currency movements.

The **effectiveness of hedging** depends on several factors, including the *accuracy of currency forecasts*, the

cost of hedging instruments, and the *investor's time horizon*. Hedging is not always cost-effective, especially for short-term investments where the cost of hedging might outweigh the potential benefit. For longer-term investments, however, hedging can provide valuable protection against substantial currency losses.

Beyond hedging, investors can also employ strategies to **reduce currency risk indirectly**. This can involve *diversifying across multiple currencies*, thereby reducing the impact of any single currency's movement. Investing in funds that employ **currency-hedged strategies** is another way to mitigate risk. These funds actively manage currency exposure, aiming to reduce or eliminate currency risk through sophisticated trading strategies. It's important to note that these funds may still be subject to some residual currency risk, however.

The decision of **whether or not to hedge** is a complex one, dependent on an investor's risk tolerance, investment horizon, and specific investment goals. Investors with a low risk tolerance and a longer-term investment horizon may find hedging particularly valuable. Conversely, investors with a higher risk tolerance and shorter-term horizons may choose to forgo hedging, accepting the potential for greater returns alongside increased risk. *Careful consideration of these factors is essential when constructing a portfolio that includes international bond funds.*

Furthermore, investors should **thoroughly research the specific funds** they are considering, paying close attention to their *currency hedging policies*, if any. Understanding the fund manager's approach to currency risk management is crucial for making informed investment decisions. Many fund prospectuses and fact sheets will clearly outline these policies, offering transparency into how the fund intends to manage this crucial aspect of international investing. Ultimately, a well-informed approach to currency risk management is critical for achieving optimal returns in the global bond market.

Finally, **consulting with a qualified financial advisor** is recommended to determine the most suitable hedging strategy based on individual circumstances and risk appetite. A financial professional can help investors navigate the complexities of currency risk and develop a comprehensive international bond portfolio aligned with their overall financial goals.

Emerging Markets vs. Developed Markets

Investing in international bond funds exposes investors to the diverse landscape of global fixed-income markets, a realm that significantly differs between emerging markets and developed markets. Understanding these distinctions is crucial for making informed investment decisions, as each presents unique opportunities and risks.

Developed markets, typically encompassing countries like the United States, Japan, and those within the European Union, are characterized by robust economies, established legal frameworks, and well-functioning capital markets. Bond issuers in these markets generally exhibit higher credit ratings and lower default risks, leading to lower yields compared to their emerging market counterparts. This stability, however, comes at the cost of potentially lower returns. Investors seeking *capital preservation* and a steady income stream often favor developed market bonds. The inherent predictability of these markets makes them attractive for conservative investors with a lower risk tolerance.

In contrast, **emerging markets**, which include countries like Brazil, China, India, and Mexico, offer a different investment proposition. These markets are characterized by higher growth potential but also carry significantly higher risk. Economic and political instability, weaker legal frameworks, and currency fluctuations are common concerns. Bond issuers in emerging markets often exhibit lower credit ratings and a greater likelihood of default. However, this increased risk can translate into higher yields to compensate investors for taking on added uncertainty. Emerging market bonds can be a compelling addition to a diversified portfolio for investors with a *higher risk tolerance* seeking potentially higher returns.

The currency risk associated with emerging market bonds is another critical factor. Fluctuations in exchange rates can significantly impact returns, especially for investors who do not hedge their currency exposure. Careful consideration of currency risk management strategies is essential when investing in international bond funds focused on emerging markets. Sophisticated investors might employ hedging techniques to mitigate this risk, but these strategies come with their own costs and complexities.

Furthermore, the political and economic climate plays a more significant role in emerging markets. Government policies, political stability, and macroeconomic factors can dramatically influence the performance of emerging market bonds. Investors need to actively monitor these factors and remain vigilant about potential risks. Geopolitical events, such as political instability or conflicts, can trigger significant market volatility in these regions.

The choice between developed and emerging market bonds depends largely on an investor's risk tolerance and investment objectives. Conservative investors seeking stability and income might prioritize developed market bonds, while investors willing to accept higher risk for potentially higher returns might allocate a portion of their portfolio to emerging market bonds. A well-diversified portfolio often includes a blend of both, allowing investors to balance risk and reward effectively. It is crucial to thoroughly research specific bond funds, understanding their underlying holdings and the risks involved before making any investment decision. Professional financial advice can prove invaluable in navigating the intricacies of international bond investing.

Ultimately, the decision of whether to invest in developed or emerging market bonds hinges on a careful assessment of one's individual circumstances, financial goals, and risk appetite. A well-informed strategy that considers both the potential rewards and inherent risks is vital for successful investing in this dynamic global marketplace.

Political and Economic Risks

Investing in international bond funds exposes investors to a unique set of challenges beyond the typical risks associated with domestic bond markets. **Political and economic risks** are intertwined and can significantly impact the performance and stability of international bond holdings. Understanding these risks is crucial for informed investment decisions.

One major concern is *political instability*. Countries with weak or unpredictable governments are prone to policy changes that can negatively affect bond markets. These changes might include unexpected tax increases, currency devaluations, or even outright defaults on government debt. **Political events**, such as elections, social unrest, or even changes in leadership, can create uncertainty and volatility, driving down bond prices. Investors need to carefully assess the political landscape of each country before investing in its bonds.

Closely related to political risk is **economic risk**. A country's economic health directly influences the value of its bonds. Factors like economic growth, inflation, and interest rates all play significant roles. A country experiencing slow economic growth or high inflation might struggle to meet its debt obligations, leading to potential defaults or credit downgrades. Similarly, unexpected shifts in monetary policy can dramatically impact bond yields and prices.

Currency risk is another critical consideration. International bond funds typically hold bonds denominated in foreign currencies. Fluctuations in exchange rates can significantly impact returns. If the value of the foreign currency declines relative to the investor's home currency, the returns from the bonds will be reduced even if the bonds themselves perform well. Hedging strategies can mitigate this risk, but they come with their own costs and complexities.

Emerging market bonds present *higher levels of political and economic risk* compared to developed markets. These economies are often more susceptible to political instability, economic shocks, and sudden policy changes. However, they also tend to offer **higher potential**

returns to compensate for the increased risk. Investors must carefully weigh the potential rewards against the significantly elevated risks before investing in emerging market bonds.

Diversification is a key strategy for managing political and economic risks in international bond investments. Spreading investments across multiple countries and regions can help reduce the impact of any single event or policy change. Additionally, thorough <u>due diligence</u> is essential. Investors should research the creditworthiness of the issuers, assess the political and economic stability of the issuing countries, and understand the potential impact of currency fluctuations before committing their capital.

In conclusion, investing in international bond funds offers the potential for diversification and higher returns, but it also exposes investors to significant political and economic risks. By carefully analyzing the political and economic landscape of each country, understanding currency risk, implementing effective diversification strategies, and employing thorough due diligence, investors can navigate these challenges and make more informed investment decisions.

Part III: Evaluating and Selecting Bond Funds and ETFs

11. Bond Fund Expenses and Fees

Expense Ratios and Management Fees

Understanding expense ratios and management fees is crucial for maximizing returns in bond funds and ETFs. These seemingly small charges can significantly impact your overall investment performance over time, quietly eroding your profits. Let's delve into the specifics of each.

Expense Ratios: The Ongoing Cost of Ownership

The expense ratio represents the annual cost of owning a bond fund or ETF, expressed as a percentage of your investment. It covers the fund's operational expenses, including management fees, administrative costs, marketing expenses, and 12b-1 fees (if applicable). A lower expense ratio generally translates to higher returns for the investor. While seemingly insignificant at first glance (e.g., 0.5% annually), these fees compound over time, becoming a substantial drain on your portfolio's potential. Imagine investing $10,000 in a fund with a 1% expense ratio; that's

$100 annually that never makes it to your investment growth, year after year.

Management Fees: Paying for Expertise (or Not)

Management fees constitute a significant portion of the expense ratio. These fees compensate the fund managers for their expertise in selecting and managing the portfolio's bonds. Active bond funds, which actively trade to outperform a benchmark, generally have higher management fees than passive bond funds (index funds and ETFs) that simply track a market index. The justification for higher fees in active funds is the potential for superior risk-adjusted returns through skillful management. However, consistently outperforming the benchmark is not guaranteed, and many active funds fail to justify their higher expense ratios over the long term.

12b-1 Fees: Marketing and Distribution Costs

Some bond funds charge 12b-1 fees, used to cover the costs of marketing and distribution. These fees are controversial, as they represent a direct deduction from investor returns to fund promotional activities rather than directly improving investment performance. While low 12b-1 fees may be acceptable, high ones should be a red flag, raising concerns about whether the fund prioritizes investor returns or marketing. Always check your fund's prospectuses carefully for these types of fees.

Transaction Costs: Hidden Expenses

Beyond the stated expense ratios and management fees, transaction costs can further impact your returns. These include brokerage commissions and market impact costs (the cost of buying or selling large volumes of bonds, pushing prices up or down). While not directly included in expense ratios, high transaction costs are more likely to eat into profits, especially in actively managed funds that engage in frequent trading. The effects of transaction costs are magnified in bond funds or ETFs with higher turnover rates. Therefore, investors should examine a fund's turnover rate to assess the extent of such costs.

Comparing Fees Across Funds

Comparing fees across different bond funds or ETFs requires careful scrutiny of the expense ratio breakdown. Don't just focus on the overall expense ratio; investigate the components. Look for funds with consistently low expense ratios and reasonable management fees. Consider that while some active management may offer potentially higher returns, it's generally more difficult to justify high management fees over the long run. Passive funds (i.e., index funds or ETFs) provide lower fees and generally better consistency, but often won't outperform the market.

The Long-Term Impact

The *cumulative effect of even small differences in expense ratios can be substantial over time.* A seemingly minor difference of 0.5% annually can drastically affect your long-term returns. This underscores the need for careful evaluation of fees before investing. The seemingly small expenses add up over time and can drastically reduce your investment growth potential. Always consider the total cost of ownership.

Conclusion

By diligently evaluating expense ratios and management fees, you can make informed decisions that optimize your bond fund and ETF investments for long-term success. Remember that lower costs contribute significantly to better long-term returns.

Transaction Costs and Other Fees

Understanding the complete cost of investing in bond funds and ETFs goes beyond simply examining the expense ratio. While the expense ratio represents the annual fee charged as a percentage of assets under management, transaction costs and other fees can significantly impact your overall returns, especially over the long term. These additional costs, often overlooked, can erode your investment gains and deserve careful scrutiny.

One significant component is **trading fees**. For actively managed bond funds, the fund manager buys and sells bonds frequently to adjust the portfolio's holdings. Each trade incurs a brokerage commission. While these individual transactions might appear insignificant, they accumulate over time. *These costs are typically absorbed by the fund itself and not explicitly charged to the investor, but they ultimately impact the fund's net asset value (NAV).* The higher the fund's trading activity, the higher the potential impact of these hidden costs.

Bond ETFs, on the other hand, generally have lower transaction costs. They are traded on exchanges like stocks, and investors pay standard brokerage commissions for buying and selling shares. However, the frequency of trading directly affects these costs. Frequent trading of an ETF to time the market will incur greater fees than buy-and-hold strategies.

Beyond trading fees, other fees can creep into your investment. These can include:

- **12b-1 fees:** These are marketing and distribution fees charged by some mutual funds. They are deducted from the fund's assets, reducing the potential return for investors. While seemingly small, these fees compound over time.

- **Account maintenance fees:** Some brokerage firms charge annual or monthly fees for maintaining an investment account. These costs are separate from the fund fees themselves but contribute to the overall investment expense.

- **Redemption fees:** Some funds may charge a fee when you sell or redeem your shares, particularly if you redeem your shares within a short period after purchase. This discourages short-term trading and helps manage fund liquidity.

- **Other charges:** These may include charges for things like account transfers, wire transfers, or other services provided by the brokerage firm or fund company.

The cumulative effect of these various costs can significantly affect your investment returns, especially over longer time horizons. A seemingly small difference in total fees across different bond funds or ETFs can translate into substantial variations in your final returns after several years. Therefore, it is crucial to carefully evaluate all fees associated with a bond fund or ETF before investing, not simply focusing solely on the expense ratio.

A **thorough analysis** requires comparing the expense ratio and these other fees for similar bond funds and ETFs. Using online resources, fund prospectuses, and brokerage statements, one can obtain the precise figures. Remember to project the cumulative impact of fees over your investment timeframe to make a well-informed decision. Careful attention to detail in this area can help you maximize the growth of your bond investments.

Impact of Fees on Long-Term Returns

The seemingly small expense ratios charged by bond funds and ETFs can have a surprisingly significant impact on your long-term returns. While these fees might appear insignificant on a yearly basis, their cumulative effect over decades of investing can dramatically reduce your overall profits. Think of it like a slow leak in a boat – a small hole might not seem problematic initially, but over time, it will sink the vessel. Similarly, seemingly minor annual fees can significantly erode your investment's growth potential.

Consider this: a fund with a 1% annual expense ratio will steadily deduct 1% of your investment's value each year. This means that if your fund earns a 5% return, your actual return after fees will be just 4%. This seemingly small difference compounds significantly over time. A <u>consistent</u>, even <u>small</u> fee, will significantly reduce the growth of your investment. To illustrate this, let's consider a hypothetical scenario. Suppose you invest $10,000 in two identical bond funds, one with a 1% expense ratio and the other with a 0.5% expense ratio. Both funds achieve an average annual return of 5% before fees over 20 years. After two decades, the fund with the 1% expense ratio would likely yield significantly less than the fund with the lower fee. This difference can be substantial, potentially representing thousands of dollars in lost earnings.

The impact of fees is particularly pronounced in the context of bond funds, which generally offer *lower* returns than equities. In contrast to higher-growth equities, where larger returns can often offset the effect of fees, the smaller returns of bond investments make fees even more impactful on your bottom line. Every basis point counts. Even a seemingly negligible difference of 0.25% between two funds can translate into substantial differences in long-term performance, particularly during periods of low interest rates, where gains are more modest.

Understanding Fee Structures:

It's crucial to understand the different types of fees associated with bond funds and ETFs. Expense ratios are the most common, covering management fees, administrative costs, and other operational expenses. However, some funds may also levy additional charges, such as front-end loads, back-end loads, or 12b-1 fees. These fees can further diminish returns and should be carefully considered when making investment decisions. The *prospectus* of each fund clearly outlines all applicable fees and charges.

The Importance of Due Diligence:

Before investing in any bond fund or ETF, thorough research is crucial. Compare the expense ratios of similar funds to determine which ones offer the most competitive pricing relative to their performance track record. Don't solely focus on past performance; consider the fund's fee structure and the potential impact of those fees on your long-term returns. A fund may boast impressive past performance, but high fees could significantly hinder its future prospects.

Furthermore, remember that seemingly minor differences in fees accumulate over time, leading to significantly larger variations in final balances. To avoid making costly mistakes, always compare not just the funds' performance history but also their **expense ratios**. Look for funds that consistently achieve strong returns while maintaining competitive fee structures. Don't let seemingly small fees become large obstacles to achieving your investment goals. The **power of compounding** works both for and against you; make sure you're using it to your advantage by selecting funds with the lowest possible fees consistent with your investment strategy and risk tolerance.

Minimizing the Impact of Fees:

While you can't entirely eliminate fees, you can significantly reduce their impact. Consider investing in low-cost index funds or ETFs that track broad bond market indexes. These passive investment vehicles typically have lower expense ratios than actively managed funds. Diversifying your bond holdings across multiple funds can also help mitigate risk, but be mindful that this strategy will not reduce your fees. Regularly review your investment portfolio and adjust it as needed, being sure to compare fees and performance across different options to determine if your current selections remain optimal. Careful attention to fees is crucial for long-term investment success.

In conclusion, the impact of fees on long-term returns in bond funds and ETFs cannot be overstated. While seemingly small, these costs compound over time, significantly affecting your overall investment growth. By carefully comparing funds, understanding fee structures, and focusing on low-cost options, you can minimize their impact and maximize your long-term returns, securing a more comfortable financial future.

12. Bond Fund Performance Analysis

Benchmarking and Relative Performance

Benchmarking and relative performance are critical aspects of evaluating bond fund success. It's not enough to simply look at a fund's raw return; you need to understand how that return stacks up against similar funds and relevant market benchmarks. This involves comparing a bond fund's performance to a designated benchmark index, which acts as a standard for measuring its success. The choice of benchmark is crucial and depends on the fund's stated investment objective. A high-yield bond fund, for example, would not be benchmarked against a government bond index because they cater to vastly different risk tolerances and investment strategies. Instead, it might be benchmarked against a broad high-yield corporate bond index or a specific sector index.

Common benchmarks include broad market indices like the Barclays Aggregate Bond Index (a broad measure of the US investment-grade bond market) or more targeted indices like the Bloomberg Barclays U.S. Corporate High Yield Index. Index selection influences the interpretation of relative performance. A fund might outperform a narrow, specialized index but underperform a broader, more diversified benchmark. The context is crucial. The key is to compare apples to apples.

Relative performance, therefore, provides context to the fund's absolute returns. A seemingly impressive 5%

return might be underwhelming if the benchmark gained 7%. Conversely, a 2% return could be seen as exceptional if the benchmark declined by 1%. This relative perspective is crucial for long-term strategic decision-making.

Analyzing relative performance involves considering several key factors:

- **Time Horizon:** Comparing short-term performance against long-term performance offers crucial insights. A short-term underperformance might be followed by impressive long-term results.

- **Expense Ratio:** A fund's expense ratio significantly impacts its returns. Two funds may have similar relative performance, but one might achieve it at a lower cost, making it the more efficient investment.

- **Risk-Adjusted Returns:** Simply comparing raw returns is insufficient. Risk-adjusted metrics like the Sharpe Ratio and Sortino Ratio consider the volatility and downside risk of a fund's returns, giving a clearer picture of its overall efficiency.

- **Standard Deviation:** A measure of volatility, standard deviation helps investors understand the fund's price fluctuations. Lower standard deviation implies lower risk, but not necessarily higher returns.

- **Beta:** This metric shows how much the fund's price fluctuates compared to the market benchmark. A beta of 1 indicates that the fund moves in line with the market; a beta greater than 1 indicates higher volatility, while a beta less than 1 suggests lower volatility.

- **Tracking Error:** For passively managed funds aiming to mirror a specific index, tracking error measures how closely the fund's performance aligns with its benchmark. A lower tracking error signifies better alignment.

By *carefully considering* these factors, investors can gain a nuanced understanding of a bond fund's performance relative to its benchmark and make more informed decisions. Remember, past performance is not indicative of future results, but a thorough analysis of relative performance provides valuable context for evaluating a fund's potential.

Furthermore, remember to consult independent rating agencies like Morningstar for additional insights. They offer comprehensive analyses of fund performance, including relative performance data alongside risk assessments and qualitative assessments of fund management strategies.

Ultimately, benchmarking and relative performance analysis is integral to successful bond fund investing, helping investors make well-informed choices aligned with their financial goals and risk tolerance.

Sharpe Ratio, Standard Deviation, and Other Risk Metrics

Understanding the risk-return profile of bond funds and ETFs is crucial for making informed investment decisions. While **return** is a straightforward concept – representing the profit generated from an investment – **risk** is multifaceted and requires a deeper understanding. Several metrics provide valuable insights into a bond fund's risk characteristics and how it balances risk and reward.

Among these, the **Sharpe Ratio**, **Standard Deviation**, and other related risk metrics play a pivotal role.

The *Standard Deviation* measures the *volatility* of a bond fund's returns. A higher standard deviation signifies greater price fluctuations over time, indicating higher risk. Conversely, a lower standard deviation suggests more stable returns, implying lower risk. It's essential to remember that while lower volatility is generally preferred, it doesn't automatically mean a better investment. The standard deviation alone doesn't capture the complete risk picture; it only shows the dispersion of returns around the average. For instance, a fund might have low volatility but still underperform its benchmark. Therefore, the standard deviation should always be considered in conjunction with other metrics.

The *Sharpe Ratio*, on the other hand, provides a more comprehensive measure of risk-adjusted return. It considers both the fund's return and its volatility relative to a risk-free rate (typically represented by the return of a government bond). The formula for the Sharpe Ratio is: *($R_p - R_f$) / σ_p*, where *R_p* is the portfolio return, *R_f* is the risk-free rate, and *σ_p* is the standard deviation of the portfolio's return. A higher Sharpe Ratio indicates better risk-adjusted performance, implying that the fund generates higher returns for each unit of risk undertaken. It essentially rewards investors who achieve higher returns without significantly increasing volatility.

Beyond the Sharpe Ratio and Standard Deviation, several other risk metrics provide further insights. **Beta** measures a fund's volatility relative to the overall market. A beta of 1 indicates that the fund moves in line with the market, while a beta greater than 1 suggests higher volatility than the market, and a beta less than 1 indicates lower volatility. **Duration** is a crucial metric for bond funds, measuring a bond portfolio's sensitivity to interest rate changes. Longer duration means higher interest rate sensitivity (and risk), while shorter duration indicates lower sensitivity. **Maximum drawdown** quantifies the largest percentage decline from a peak to a trough in a fund's value over a specific period. This metric helps gauge a fund's resilience during market downturns. Finally, **Sortino Ratio** is similar to the Sharpe Ratio but focuses only on downside risk (losses), making it a more refined measure for risk-averse investors.

Understanding these various risk metrics is not merely an academic exercise; it is essential for constructing a well-diversified and risk-appropriate bond portfolio. Investors should carefully analyze the risk profiles of different bond funds and ETFs, considering their individual risk tolerance and investment objectives. The appropriate use of these metrics ensures a more robust and informed investment strategy, ultimately enhancing the likelihood of achieving long-term investment goals.

Remember, no single metric tells the whole story. It's imperative to consider several risk metrics in conjunction with return data and qualitative factors, such as fund manager expertise and market conditions, for a complete assessment.

Morningstar Ratings and Other Independent Ratings

Independent ratings services play a crucial role in helping investors navigate the complex world of bond funds. These ratings provide a valuable, albeit imperfect, snapshot of a fund's past performance, risk profile, and overall quality. While not a guaranteed predictor of future returns, they offer a standardized framework for comparison and analysis, helping investors make more informed decisions. Among the most widely recognized names is Morningstar, a behemoth in the financial research industry. Their ratings system provides a comprehensive assessment, incorporating various factors beyond simple performance numbers.

Morningstar's star rating system, for example, is arguably the most familiar metric used by individual investors. This system, ranging from one to five stars, isn't solely based on a fund's return; it also accounts for risk-adjusted performance, expense ratios, and manager tenure. A five-star rating signifies consistently superior performance relative to its peers after adjusting for risk. However, investors should understand that past performance is not necessarily indicative of future results. A fund might receive a high star rating based on past achievements but could underperform in the future due to changing market conditions or shifts in investment strategies.

Beyond Morningstar's star ratings, their analytical reports provide a more in-depth evaluation. These reports delve into a fund's portfolio holdings, investment approach, and management team. They also offer insights into the fund's expense ratio, which is a critical factor impacting long-term returns. **Understanding a fund's expense ratio is paramount**; even seemingly small differences can accumulate significantly over time, potentially eroding your returns. Morningstar's reports help investors compare expense ratios across different funds, facilitating more cost-effective investment choices.

Other independent rating agencies, such as Lipper and Standard & Poor's, offer similar rating systems and analytical reports, though their methodologies and emphasis might vary slightly. These agencies provide different perspectives and methodologies, allowing investors to obtain a more holistic understanding of a fund's strengths and weaknesses. It's essential for investors to *consult multiple rating sources* to gain a well-rounded perspective, rather than solely relying on a single rating.

However, it is crucial to remember that these ratings are just one piece of the puzzle. Investors should not make investment decisions solely based on ratings. Thorough due diligence remains essential. This includes **carefully reviewing the fund's prospectus, understanding its investment strategy and objectives**, and **assessing the fund manager's expertise and track record**. The ratings provide a valuable starting point for analysis, but they should not be the sole factor influencing investment decisions.

In conclusion, Morningstar ratings and other independent ratings offer valuable guidance, providing a structured framework for comparing bond funds. However, investors should use these ratings judiciously, complementing them with a comprehensive understanding of the fund's investment strategy, expense ratios, risk profile, and manager expertise. A well-informed approach, combining independent research with careful analysis, allows investors to select bond funds that best align with their individual financial goals and risk tolerance.

13. Bond Fund Ratings and Research

Using Independent Ratings to Assess Risk

Independent ratings agencies play a crucial role in the bond market, providing investors with an objective assessment of the creditworthiness of bond issuers and the inherent risk associated with different bond funds. Understanding these ratings is paramount for making informed investment decisions. This section delves into the significance of independent ratings, how they are used to gauge risk, and the limitations investors should be aware of.

The Role of Rating Agencies: Major rating agencies, such as Moody's, Standard & Poor's (S&P), and Fitch, meticulously analyze the financial health and creditworthiness of bond issuers. Their analyses consider various factors, including a company's profitability, debt levels, cash flow, management quality, and industry outlook. These assessments are then translated into letter-based ratings, with higher ratings indicating lower risk and vice-versa.

Interpreting Bond Ratings: Investment-grade bonds typically receive ratings of AAA to BBB- (or equivalent ratings from other agencies). These bonds are considered relatively safe, with a lower likelihood of default. Conversely, high-yield bonds (also known as junk bonds) have ratings below BB+ and are associated with higher default risk. The higher the rating, the lower the perceived

102

risk and, generally, the lower the yield offered. It is important to note that ratings are not static; they can change over time as the financial health of the issuer fluctuates.

Using Ratings to Assess Fund Risk: Independent ratings are not only applied to individual bonds but also to bond funds themselves. Rating agencies assess a bond fund's overall risk profile based on the underlying portfolio's holdings. This provides investors with a broader perspective on the fund's risk exposure. A highly-rated fund suggests that the fund manager has strategically selected bonds with minimal credit risk. However, it is important to note that even a well-rated fund can still face market risk (such as interest rate fluctuations).

Beyond the Rating: While independent ratings are a valuable tool, investors should avoid relying solely on them. It's crucial to perform your own due diligence, considering factors such as the *fund's investment strategy, expense ratio, past performance (keeping in mind past performance is not indicative of future results), and the fund manager's expertise.* Moreover, it is essential to remember that rating agencies are not infallible; their assessments are based on available information and may not always perfectly predict future outcomes.

Different Rating Scales: It's important to remember that different rating agencies use slightly different rating scales and methodologies. Understanding the nuances of these differences can provide a more comprehensive understanding of a bond's or fund's risk profile. Comparing ratings across different agencies can offer a more robust perspective on the creditworthiness of the investment.

Limitations of Ratings: It's crucial to acknowledge the limitations of bond ratings. Ratings are backward-looking, primarily reflecting historical data. They may not adequately predict future changes in an issuer's financial condition or the impact of unforeseen events. Additionally, rating agencies are not immune to biases or conflicts of interest.

Active vs. Passive Management and Ratings: The type of fund management (active or passive) also affects how ratings are interpreted. Actively managed bond funds aim to outperform their benchmarks, and their ratings reflect their overall risk assessment taking into account the manager's active strategies. Passively managed funds, which aim to track a specific bond index, have ratings that reflect the inherent risk of the underlying index.

Conclusion: Independent ratings provide a valuable, albeit imperfect, tool for assessing the risk associated with bond funds. They offer a structured framework for comparing the relative risk of different investments. However, investors should treat these ratings as one factor among many when making their investment decisions, considering other relevant factors mentioned above for a well-rounded assessment of risk and potential return.

Analyzing Fund Manager Track Records

Assessing the track record of a bond fund manager is crucial for discerning the fund's potential for future performance. While past performance is *not* a guarantee of future results, a thorough examination of historical data can reveal valuable insights into a manager's investment philosophy, skill, and risk management approach. This analysis shouldn't be a simple glance at a few numbers;

rather, it requires a multi-faceted approach that considers several key aspects.

First and foremost, <u>consider the manager's tenure</u>. A manager with a long and consistent track record demonstrates experience and stability. Look beyond just total returns and delve into their performance during different market cycles. How did the fund perform during periods of rising interest rates, economic recessions, or market volatility? A manager who consistently delivers positive returns even during challenging times showcases superior risk management and a robust investment strategy. Conversely, a manager with a short tenure or a history of inconsistent performance might present greater risk.

Benchmarking is another essential element. How has the fund performed relative to its benchmark index? While outperformance is desirable, a manager who consistently beats the benchmark while taking on excessive risk might not be a suitable choice for all investors. Conversely, a manager who underperforms the benchmark might require closer scrutiny to understand the reasons behind the underperformance. Was it due to a deliberate, calculated strategy, or a lack of skill and foresight? Analyzing the fund's alpha and beta can provide further context. Alpha reflects the manager's skill in generating returns above the benchmark, while beta measures the fund's volatility relative to the market.

Next, examine the fund's *investment strategy* and how it aligns with the manager's track record. Does the historical performance reflect the stated investment objective? For instance, a fund claiming a low-risk, conservative approach should have a track record that supports this assertion. Discrepancies between stated strategy and actual performance are red flags that require further investigation.

Furthermore, don't overlook the **fund's turnover rate**. A high turnover rate indicates frequent buying and selling of bonds, which can lead to higher transaction costs and potentially erode returns. Understanding the rationale behind the manager's trading activity is essential. Is the high turnover a reflection of a dynamic, opportunistic strategy or simply excessive trading that adds unnecessary expenses?

Finally, consider the *manager's investment team* and the firm's resources. A strong research team, access to sophisticated analytical tools, and a well-defined investment process can significantly enhance the manager's ability to deliver consistent returns. Researching the firm's history, reputation, and commitment to responsible investing will provide a comprehensive picture.

In conclusion, analyzing a bond fund manager's track record involves more than just reviewing past returns. It requires a holistic approach that considers market cycles, benchmark performance, investment strategy alignment, turnover rate, and the overall resources and expertise of the management team. This detailed analysis will empower investors to make informed decisions and select bond funds aligned with their investment goals and risk tolerance.

Reading Fund Fact Sheets

Fund fact sheets are **indispensable tools** for navigating the complex world of bond funds. These concise documents provide a snapshot of a fund's key characteristics, performance, and holdings, allowing investors to make informed decisions. Mastering the art of reading fact sheets is crucial for success in bond investing. Don't just glance at them; *actively dissect each section* to extract meaningful information.

Begin by examining the **fund's objective**. This clearly states the fund's investment strategy, such as focusing on short-term bonds, high-yield securities, or a specific sector. Understanding the objective is paramount as it sets the stage for interpreting other data presented. Next, pay close attention to the **fund's investment strategy**, which provides further detail on how the fund manager aims to achieve the stated objective. This may include specific sectors, asset classes, and risk tolerance levels.

The **fund's performance data** is another crucial component. Fact sheets typically present historical performance figures, including returns over various periods (e.g., 1 year, 3 years, 5 years, 10 years). It is critical, however, to consider these figures within the context of the fund's stated objective and benchmark. A high-yield bond fund, for instance, is expected to have higher volatility than a government bond fund. Comparing performance against a relevant benchmark helps gauge whether the fund is achieving its goal effectively. Do not focus solely on past performance, however; it is *no guarantee of future returns*.

A detailed analysis of the **fund's holdings** offers invaluable insight. Fact sheets typically provide a breakdown of the fund's asset allocation across different bond types (e.g., government bonds, corporate bonds, municipal bonds), maturities, and credit ratings. This information is vital for assessing the fund's risk profile and potential for returns. For example, a fund heavily weighted in long-term bonds will be more sensitive to interest rate changes than one focused on short-term bonds. The **sector**

breakdown can highlight any undue concentration in specific sectors, which may increase the fund's vulnerability to industry-specific risks.

Expense ratios are a significant factor influencing a bond fund's long-term performance. Fact sheets clearly state the annual expense ratio, which represents the annual cost of owning the fund as a percentage of its assets. Lower expense ratios generally translate to higher returns for investors. Compare the expense ratio with those of similar funds to ensure that the fund's fees are competitive.

Finally, always review the **fund's manager's experience and investment philosophy**. This section provides insight into the fund management team's expertise and approach to investing. A well-established team with a consistent and transparent investment philosophy often signals greater confidence. The fact sheet might also offer information on the manager's track record, although past performance, as always, is not necessarily indicative of future results.

In conclusion, *thoroughly reading and understanding fund fact sheets* is an essential part of successful bond investing. By diligently analyzing the information provided, investors can make well-informed decisions that align with their investment objectives and risk tolerance.

14. Bond Fund Dividends and Distributions

Tax Implications of Bond Fund Dividends

Understanding the tax implications of bond fund dividends is crucial for maximizing your investment returns. The tax treatment of these dividends hinges primarily on the type of bond held within the fund and your individual tax bracket. Let's delve into the complexities.

Interest Income from Investment-Grade Bonds: Dividends stemming from investment-grade corporate bonds and government bonds are generally taxed as ordinary income. This means they're taxed at your marginal tax rate – the highest rate applicable to your income level. This is a straightforward aspect, but the overall tax liability can be significant for higher-income investors.

Municipal Bond Interest: A key advantage of municipal bond funds is the potential for tax-exempt income. Interest earned on municipal bonds is generally exempt from federal income tax, and often from state and local taxes as well, if the bonds are issued within your state of residence. This feature makes municipal bond funds particularly appealing to investors in higher tax brackets, as it can significantly reduce their overall tax burden. However, it's vital to note that not all municipal bonds are created equal. The tax-exempt status can vary based on the specific bonds held within the fund.

High-Yield Bond (Junk Bond) Interest: High-yield bond funds, while potentially offering higher returns, come with increased risk. The interest income from these bonds is also treated as ordinary income, subject to your marginal tax rate. While the higher yield may initially seem attractive, remember to factor in the increased risk and the potential impact of higher taxes on your net return.

Capital Gains Distributions: Bond funds may also distribute capital gains to investors. These gains occur when the fund sells bonds at a profit. Capital gains distributions are taxed at preferential capital gains rates, which are generally lower than ordinary income tax rates. However, the exact rate depends on your income level and the holding period of the bonds within the fund. Long-term capital gains (bonds held for more than one year) typically have lower rates than short-term gains.

Tax-Efficient Strategies: To mitigate your tax liability, consider these strategies:

- **Tax-loss harvesting:** If a bond fund incurs losses, consider using tax-loss harvesting to offset capital gains from other investments.
- **Tax-advantaged accounts:** Investing in bond funds within tax-advantaged accounts like 401(k)s or IRAs can defer or eliminate taxes on dividends and capital gains.
- **Fund Selection:** Choose funds with a history of lower capital gains distributions if minimizing tax liabilities is a priority. Note, however, that this may mean sacrificing some potential returns.

Record Keeping: Meticulous record-keeping is crucial. Your fund company will provide you with a tax statement at the end of the year, detailing the distributions and their tax characteristics. Keep this information organized and readily accessible for tax preparation. Failure to properly document distributions can lead to unnecessary tax penalties.

Professional Advice: The tax implications of bond fund dividends can be complex. For personalized guidance tailored to your specific financial situation and tax bracket, consult with a qualified financial advisor or tax professional. They can help you optimize your investment strategy to minimize your tax burden while maximizing your returns.

Disclaimer: This information is for educational purposes only and does not constitute financial or tax advice. Consult with a qualified professional before making any investment decisions.

Reinvestment Options

Understanding reinvestment options is crucial for maximizing returns and managing the tax implications of your bond fund investments. Most bond funds offer a variety of reinvestment choices, allowing you to control how your distributions are handled. The key lies in selecting the option that best aligns with your financial goals and risk tolerance. *Let's delve into the common reinvestment options available to bond fund investors:*

Automatic Reinvestment: This is the most popular choice. Distributions, including interest and capital gains, are automatically reinvested into additional shares of the fund. This strategy fosters compounding growth, as your earnings generate further earnings over time. The power of compounding is significant in the long run, significantly enhancing your overall returns. However, this option doesn't provide immediate cash flow.

Cash Distribution: Conversely, opting for cash distribution means you receive your dividends and capital gains directly into your brokerage account as cash. This provides immediate liquidity, which is beneficial for meeting short-term financial needs or expenses. *However, this approach may hinder long-term growth* due to the absence of compounding. You lose the opportunity for those dividends to buy more shares at potentially lower prices. Tax implications are also immediate.

Dividend Reinvestment Plan (DRIP): Some bond funds offer a dedicated DRIP, often with a lower minimum investment requirement. This plan enables you to reinvest dividends automatically, even if only a small amount, contributing to steady growth. **DRIPs are especially advantageous for long-term investors aiming for consistent accumulation**.

Partial Reinvestment: A flexible option is to partially reinvest your distributions. You can choose to reinvest a specific percentage of your earnings while taking the rest as cash. This allows for a balance between immediate liquidity and compounding growth. For example, reinvesting 75% while keeping 25% allows some cash flow while still maximizing your returns.

Tax Implications: The tax consequences of your reinvestment decision can significantly impact your overall returns. Reinvesting distributions defers the tax liability, allowing your earnings to grow tax-free until you sell your shares. Cash distributions, however, are immediately taxable, and may influence your tax bracket for the year.

Consult a tax professional to tailor your reinvestment strategy according to your personal circumstances.

Choosing the Right Option: The optimal reinvestment approach depends largely on your individual investment goals and timeline. **Long-term investors focused on wealth building will usually favor automatic reinvestment or DRIPs.** Those requiring regular income might prefer cash distributions or partial reinvestment. *Carefully consider your risk tolerance, tax implications, and liquidity needs before making your decision.* Regularly review your chosen approach to ensure it still aligns with your evolving financial objectives.

Ultimately, understanding and strategically utilizing reinvestment options is paramount to making your bond fund investments work effectively for you. It allows for a tailored approach that optimizes growth while managing cash flow and tax responsibilities. Remember to stay informed and adapt your strategy as your circumstances change.

Managing Tax Liability

Understanding the tax implications of bond fund investments is crucial for maximizing your returns and minimizing your tax burden. Bond fund distributions, whether they are interest income or capital gains, are taxable events. The type of bond fund you invest in significantly impacts the nature and timing of these taxable distributions. For instance, **municipal bond funds** generally offer tax-exempt income at the federal level, although state and local taxes may still apply depending on your residency. This makes them particularly attractive for high-income individuals in high-tax states. In contrast,

corporate and government bond funds distribute interest income that's taxable at both the federal and potentially state levels.

Capital gains distributions from bond funds are also a significant tax consideration. These arise when the fund sells bonds at a profit. The timing of these distributions can be unpredictable and can vary considerably depending on the fund's trading strategy. Unlike interest income, which is generally received regularly, capital gains distributions are typically made annually or less frequently. This can lead to tax liability surprises if not properly anticipated. Funds might distribute capital gains even if you haven't sold any shares yourself, as this distribution reflects the fund's overall performance.

Effective tax management requires careful planning and an understanding of your individual tax bracket. Tax-sheltered accounts, like *401(k)s* and *IRAs*, can be powerful tools for mitigating the tax implications of bond fund investments. Contributions to these accounts are often tax-deductible, and the growth within the accounts is tax-deferred, meaning you only pay taxes upon withdrawal. This strategy is particularly useful for long-term investors looking to build wealth over many years. However, remember that withdrawal rules apply to these accounts, which need to be carefully considered when determining the best strategy.

Tax-loss harvesting is another sophisticated strategy that can help offset tax liabilities. If you hold bond funds that have experienced losses, you can sell them to generate capital losses which can be used to offset capital gains from other investments. However, this involves intricate tax regulations and requires careful timing to avoid triggering any unintended tax consequences. It's often advisable to seek professional tax advice before implementing such a strategy.

Beyond individual tax brackets, the tax implications also depend on the specific type of bond within a bond fund. **Treasury Inflation-Protected Securities (TIPS)**, for example, may have unique tax considerations, as their returns incorporate inflation adjustments. Similarly, the structure of a bond fund, such as whether it's an open-end or closed-end fund, could also subtly influence how and when taxes are assessed. Open-end funds, which are more common, allow investors to buy and sell shares directly with the fund, whereas closed-end funds trade on exchanges like stocks.

Finally, <u>diversification</u> across different bond fund types can help spread out tax liabilities over time. By combining tax-advantaged funds with taxable funds, investors can potentially create a more tax-efficient portfolio tailored to their specific circumstances. It is always recommended to consult with a qualified financial advisor and tax professional to develop a comprehensive tax strategy that aligns with your overall financial goals and risk tolerance. They can provide personalized advice and insights that consider your specific situation and help you navigate the complexities of tax planning for bond fund investments.

Remember, proactive tax management is not just about minimizing your current tax bill; it's also about optimizing your long-term financial health. A well-structured bond portfolio, considering both investment goals and tax efficiency, is crucial for building lasting wealth.

15. Building a Bond Portfolio with ETFs and Funds

Diversification Strategies

Building a robust and resilient bond portfolio hinges significantly on employing effective diversification strategies. This isn't simply about spreading your investments across different bond funds; it's a nuanced approach that considers various factors to mitigate risk and optimize returns. A well-diversified portfolio should aim to reduce the impact of any single investment's underperformance, protecting your overall investment from significant losses.

Diversification Across Bond Types: The most fundamental strategy involves diversifying across different types of bonds. This includes incorporating **government bonds** (offering relative stability), **corporate bonds** (providing potential for higher returns but with increased risk), and **municipal bonds** (offering tax advantages). Within each category, further diversification is crucial. For example, within corporate bonds, consider including bonds from various sectors (e.g., technology, healthcare, finance) and credit ratings (investment-grade and high-yield). This approach reduces your reliance on the performance of any specific sector or credit quality.

Diversification by Maturity: Managing interest rate risk is paramount. **Maturity diversification** involves holding bonds with varying maturities – from short-term to long-term. This approach balances the trade-off between capital preservation (short-term bonds) and capital appreciation (long-term bonds). A balanced portfolio might include a mix of short-term, intermediate-term, and long-term bonds, reducing the impact of interest rate fluctuations on your overall portfolio value. The ideal allocation depends on your risk tolerance and investment horizon.

Geographic Diversification: For investors seeking broader exposure, **international bond funds** offer diversification beyond domestic markets. This strategy mitigates risk associated with economic downturns in a single country. However, it's essential to acknowledge the added complexity of currency fluctuations and geopolitical risks. Careful research and potentially employing currency hedging strategies are important considerations when investing internationally.

Active vs. Passive Management Diversification: The choice between active and passive bond funds also plays a role in diversification. **Active bond funds** aim to outperform benchmarks by actively managing their portfolios, while **passive bond funds** (like bond ETFs tracking indices) aim to mirror the performance of a specific bond index. Combining both approaches can offer a blend of active management's potential for higher returns and the lower expense ratios often associated with passive funds.

Issuer Diversification: Within each bond type, diversifying across multiple issuers is critical. This reduces the impact of a single issuer's default or financial distress. For example, rather than concentrating heavily in bonds issued by a single corporation, spread your investments across numerous corporations of varying sizes and industries. This minimizes the potential losses from the failure of a single entity.

Diversification Through ETFs: Bond exchange-traded funds (ETFs) offer a convenient and cost-effective way to achieve diversification. Many ETFs provide exposure to a broad range of bonds, making it easy to create a diversified portfolio with a single investment. This is particularly useful for investors with smaller capital sums who may struggle to achieve sufficient diversification through individual bond purchases.

Regular Rebalancing: Once you've established your diversified portfolio, it's essential to **rebalance** it periodically. This involves adjusting your asset allocations to maintain your target percentages for each bond category. Rebalancing helps to lock in profits from outperforming investments and reinvest in underperforming areas, maintaining your long-term strategy and risk profile.

Ultimately, *effective diversification is not a one-size-fits-all solution.* The optimal strategy depends heavily on individual investor circumstances, including risk tolerance, time horizon, and financial goals. Consulting a financial advisor can help you tailor a diversification strategy that aligns with your unique needs and investment objectives.

Asset Allocation Based on Risk Tolerance

Crafting an effective bond portfolio necessitates a deep understanding of your personal risk tolerance. This isn't simply about choosing between high-yield or investment-grade funds; it's about aligning your investment strategy with your comfort level regarding potential losses.

Risk tolerance is a subjective measure, reflecting your ability and willingness to accept market fluctuations in pursuit of potentially higher returns. A *conservative investor*, for instance, prioritizes capital preservation and will generally favor lower-risk options, even if it means accepting potentially lower returns. Conversely, a *growth-oriented investor* might be more comfortable with higher-risk investments, hoping to achieve significantly greater returns.

Several factors influence an individual's risk tolerance. **Time horizon** plays a crucial role. Investors with longer time horizons (e.g., those saving for retirement decades in the future) can generally tolerate more risk because they have time to recover from potential market downturns. Conversely, those nearing retirement or needing funds soon will prioritize capital preservation and likely choose less volatile bond funds and ETFs.

Your **financial situation** is another key determinant. If you have substantial assets beyond your bond portfolio, you might feel more comfortable taking on additional risk. However, those with limited financial resources will likely prefer a more conservative strategy. Personal circumstances, such as outstanding debt or dependents, can also impact risk tolerance. Someone with considerable debt obligations may opt for a less risky investment approach to ensure their debt is managed effectively.

The **asset allocation** strategy itself should directly reflect your risk tolerance. A conservative investor might allocate a significant portion of their bond portfolio to short-term, investment-grade government bonds, prioritizing stability and predictability. Such an allocation minimizes risk, but also results in potentially lower returns. A moderate risk tolerance would involve a more diversified approach, incorporating a blend of short-term and long-term, investment-grade and potentially some higher-yield bonds. This strategy aims to achieve a balance between risk and return.

On the other hand, *aggressive investors* with a high risk tolerance and longer time horizons might incorporate a larger proportion of higher-yield corporate bonds and emerging market debt into their portfolios. This strategy could yield potentially higher returns but also carries the risk of larger losses. This segment might even consider allocating a portion to actively managed bond funds to take advantage of potential alpha generation – though this carries its own set of risks related to management fees and expertise.

Determining your appropriate **risk profile** is a crucial step. Many financial institutions provide online questionnaires or consultations to help assess this. Understanding your tolerance for potential losses helps guide your choice of specific bond funds and ETFs, ensuring your investments are aligned with your long-term financial goals and comfort level.

Remember that **regular rebalancing** is crucial. As market conditions change, your portfolio's allocation might drift away from your target asset allocation. Regular rebalancing helps to maintain your desired risk exposure over time, ensuring your portfolio continues to align with your risk tolerance. This is especially important after periods of significant market volatility where certain asset classes may have performed exceptionally well or poorly, upsetting your initial balance.

Ultimately, asset allocation based on risk tolerance is a personalized process. There is no one-size-fits-all solution.

Carefully considering your circumstances, financial goals, and comfort level with risk is essential for building a bond portfolio that meets your needs and contributes to your long-term financial success. Seeking professional financial advice can be invaluable in navigating this process and developing a comprehensive investment plan.

Rebalancing Strategies

Rebalancing your bond portfolio, whether comprised of funds or ETFs, is a crucial aspect of long-term investment success. It's not just about passively watching your investments grow; it's an active strategy to maintain your desired **asset allocation** and manage **risk**. Over time, market fluctuations will cause the proportions of your holdings to drift from your original plan. Rebalancing systematically corrects these deviations, bringing your portfolio back into alignment with your **risk tolerance** and **financial goals**.

There are several key rebalancing strategies, each with its own merits and considerations:

Time-Based Rebalancing:

This approach involves rebalancing your portfolio at predetermined intervals, such as annually, semi-annually, or quarterly. The frequency depends on your **risk tolerance** and the **volatility** of your holdings. More frequent rebalancing is suitable for investors with a lower risk tolerance, as it helps to control potential losses during market downturns. Conversely, less frequent rebalancing may be appropriate for long-term investors with higher risk tolerance who are less concerned with short-term fluctuations.

Percentage-Based Rebalancing:

This method involves rebalancing when the allocation of your assets deviates from your target percentages by a certain threshold. For instance, you might rebalance when a specific asset class, such as high-yield bonds, drifts more than 5% from its target allocation. This approach is more responsive to market movements than time-based rebalancing, ensuring that your portfolio remains closely aligned with your target allocation, thereby minimizing risk.

Threshold Rebalancing:

This is a hybrid approach that combines elements of both time-based and percentage-based strategies. You might rebalance annually, but only if the deviation from your target allocation exceeds a predetermined threshold (e.g., 3% or 5%). This strategy provides flexibility, allowing for rebalancing only when necessary while maintaining a disciplined approach to portfolio management.

Considerations When Rebalancing:

Several factors should be considered when developing your rebalancing strategy. These include:

- **Transaction Costs:** Frequent rebalancing can lead to higher transaction costs, particularly if you are trading individual bonds. For bond funds and ETFs, the costs are generally lower, but still relevant.
- **Tax Implications:** Selling bonds to rebalance may trigger capital gains taxes. This is particularly important for taxable accounts. Consider tax-

efficient strategies and the tax implications of various bond funds and ETFs.

- **Market Timing:** While rebalancing is not market timing, it's important to be mindful of potential market downturns and to avoid making emotional decisions.
- **Investment Objectives:** Your rebalancing strategy should align with your overall investment objectives and risk tolerance.

Conclusion: Rebalancing is a powerful tool for managing risk and achieving long-term investment success in the bond market. By implementing a well-defined rebalancing strategy, investors can maintain their desired asset allocation, potentially reducing volatility and improving overall portfolio performance. The choice of strategy should be tailored to individual circumstances, risk tolerance, and investment goals, considering factors such as transaction costs and tax implications. Careful consideration and disciplined execution are key to effective rebalancing.

Part IV: Advanced Strategies and Considerations

16. Using Bond Funds and ETFs in Retirement Planning

Generating Income in Retirement

Retirement planning is a multifaceted endeavor, and a critical component is securing a reliable stream of income to sustain your lifestyle. While Social Security and pensions play a role for many, they often fall short of covering all expenses. This is where strategically utilizing bond funds and ETFs can become invaluable, providing a stable and potentially growing income source during your golden years. The key lies in understanding the various types of bond funds, their risk profiles, and how they can be incorporated into a well-diversified retirement portfolio.

High-Yield Bond Funds: A Higher-Risk, Higher-Reward Approach

High-yield, or junk, bond funds invest in corporate bonds rated below investment grade. These bonds offer the potential for higher yields compared to investment-grade bonds, boosting your retirement income. However, they come with significantly increased default risk. The potential for missed payments or even principal loss makes them a less suitable choice for risk-averse retirees. Careful consideration of your risk tolerance and the diversification of your overall portfolio is crucial before including high-yield bond funds.

Investment-Grade Corporate Bond Funds: Balancing Income and Stability

Investment-grade corporate bonds, rated Baa3/BBB- or higher, represent a more conservative approach to generating retirement income. These funds offer a relatively stable income stream while mitigating the higher default risk associated with high-yield bonds. However, their yields are typically lower than high-yield options, so investors need to balance their income needs against their risk appetite. The diversity within this sector allows for strategic choices based on factors like maturity dates and industry exposure.

Government Bond Funds: The Foundation of Secure Retirement Income

Government bond funds, particularly those investing in U.S. Treasury securities, provide the bedrock of stability for retirement income. These bonds are backed by the full faith and credit of the government, making them extremely low-risk. While yields may be lower than corporate bonds, the security they offer is invaluable for retirees who prioritize capital preservation. Different maturities of Treasury securities (bills, notes, bonds) allow for adjustments based on desired income streams and interest rate sensitivity.

Municipal Bond Funds: Tax Advantages for Retirement Income

Municipal bond funds offer a compelling combination of income generation and tax advantages. The interest earned on municipal bonds is often exempt from federal income taxes, and sometimes state and local taxes as well. This feature significantly boosts the after-tax return, making them an attractive option for retirees in higher tax brackets. However, it's crucial to understand the creditworthiness of the municipal issuers and the potential risks associated with specific types of municipal bonds (general obligation vs. revenue bonds).

Strategic Asset Allocation and Rebalancing

A successful retirement income strategy doesn't rely on a single type of bond fund. Diversification is key. A well-structured portfolio might include a mix of investment-grade corporate bonds for stability, a smaller allocation to high-yield bonds for enhanced returns (if appropriate for your risk profile), and a core position in government bonds for security. Regular rebalancing ensures that your portfolio remains aligned with your risk tolerance and income goals over time. This proactive approach helps manage potential downturns and safeguards your retirement income stream.

Laddered Portfolios and Income Sequencing

To optimize income streams, many retirees use laddered portfolios. This strategy involves owning bonds with a range of maturities, ensuring a regular flow of principal repayments that can be reinvested or used for income. Similarly, income sequencing involves strategically drawing down on principal to meet income needs, prioritizing principal preservation in the earlier years of retirement.

Professional Guidance

Navigating the complexities of bond funds and ETFs can be challenging. Consider seeking guidance from a *financial advisor* experienced in retirement planning. They can help you create a personalized strategy that aligns with your unique circumstances, risk tolerance, and income objectives, ensuring a secure and comfortable retirement.

In conclusion, bond funds and ETFs offer valuable tools for generating retirement income. By understanding the different types of bond funds, their associated risks, and implementing strategic asset allocation and rebalancing, retirees can create a stable and potentially growing income stream to support their lifestyle in retirement. Remember to factor in your risk tolerance and seek professional advice to tailor a plan to your specific needs.

Managing Risk in Retirement

Retirement, a period often envisioned as a time of relaxation and enjoyment, requires careful financial planning to ensure its sustainability. A significant aspect of this planning revolves around managing risk. While aiming for growth in your investments, preserving your capital and ensuring a steady income stream are paramount. Bond funds and ETFs, with their inherent characteristics, offer valuable tools for mitigating various risks associated with retirement portfolios.

One major risk is *inflation*. The eroding power of money necessitates strategies that protect against inflation's impact on your purchasing power. Inflation-protected securities (TIPS), often found within government bond funds, provide a hedge against inflation by adjusting their principal value based on inflation rates. Diversifying your bond holdings across different types, including TIPS and potentially those with inflation-linked features, can offer greater resilience to inflation's damaging effects during your retirement years. This helps ensure your retirement income maintains its value over time.

Another critical risk is *interest rate risk*. Rising interest rates can diminish the value of existing bonds, impacting your portfolio's overall worth. To counter this, incorporating short-term bond funds into your retirement portfolio can significantly reduce your vulnerability to interest rate fluctuations. Short-term bonds have shorter maturities, meaning their prices are less susceptible to interest rate changes than long-term bonds. This helps create a more stable foundation for your retirement income stream, minimizing unexpected losses.

Sequence of returns risk is particularly relevant for retirees. Negative returns early in retirement can severely impact the longevity of your savings. A conservative approach, utilizing low-risk bond funds alongside a smaller allocation to equities, can mitigate this risk. The stability offered by bond funds helps to protect against significant drawdowns, allowing you to weather market downturns without drastically depleting your retirement nest egg. This provides psychological reassurance and reduces the anxiety often associated with market volatility during retirement.

For those seeking a higher yield while still maintaining a degree of safety, high-yield bond funds might seem appealing. However, it's crucial to carefully consider the inherent risks. High-yield bonds carry a greater risk of default, which can lead to capital losses. The inclusion of high-yield bonds should be carefully planned and only considered if the investor has a high risk tolerance and a longer time horizon, it is not typically recommended as a large part of a retirement portfolio where capital preservation is a high priority.

Diversification is a cornerstone of risk management. Spreading your investments across various bond types, including government, corporate, and municipal bonds, reduces your dependence on any single sector's performance. Utilizing *bond ETFs* can facilitate efficient diversification, offering exposure to a wide range of bonds within a single investment. This diversification approach helps to mitigate systemic risks and improve the overall resilience of your retirement portfolio to unforeseen economic shocks.

Beyond the inherent risks of the bond market itself, managing your withdrawal strategy is paramount. A well-defined withdrawal plan that carefully considers your expenses, life expectancy, and investment performance is essential. It's crucial to avoid overly aggressive withdrawals that could deplete your savings prematurely. Consulting with a financial advisor can help you develop a personalized withdrawal strategy tailored to your specific circumstances and risk tolerance, ensuring you receive a dependable income stream throughout your retirement.

In conclusion, managing risk in retirement requires a multifaceted approach. Utilizing the diverse range of bond funds and ETFs available, understanding the various types of risks associated with different investment vehicles, and implementing a well-structured withdrawal plan are essential elements of ensuring your retirement savings remain secure and provide a sustainable income for many years to come. Careful consideration of these factors will help ensure a comfortable and secure retirement.

Tax-Efficient Strategies

Investing in bond funds and ETFs offers several avenues for **tax-efficient** strategies, crucial for maximizing your returns and minimizing your tax burden. Understanding these strategies is particularly important for higher-income individuals and those in higher tax brackets. The key lies in leveraging the characteristics of different bond types and fund structures to optimize your tax position.

One primary area to consider is the **type of bond** within your portfolio. Municipal bonds, for instance, offer a significant advantage. The interest earned on municipal bonds is generally exempt from federal income tax, and often from state and local taxes as well, if the bonds are issued within your state of residence. This makes them particularly attractive for investors in higher tax brackets, as the tax savings can substantially boost their after-tax returns. Investing in *municipal bond funds* or ETFs provides diversified exposure to this tax-advantaged asset class.

Another important consideration is the **tax treatment of distributions**. Bond funds, both actively and passively managed, may distribute income to their shareholders in the form of interest payments. These distributions are taxable as ordinary income in the year they are received. Therefore, understanding the *tax implications* of these distributions is vital for tax planning. It's essential to carefully review a fund's prospectus to understand its typical distribution policy and its potential tax consequences.

For investors holding bond funds within **tax-advantaged accounts** such as 401(k)s, IRAs, or Roth IRAs, the tax implications are significantly different. Within these accounts, the growth and income generated by bond funds are generally tax-deferred (until retirement for traditional accounts or completely tax-free for Roth accounts), providing substantial tax savings over the long term. This allows your investments to compound tax-free, maximizing their potential.

Moreover, the choice between **actively managed and passively managed bond funds** can impact your tax efficiency. Actively managed funds, which aim to outperform a benchmark, may generate higher capital gains distributions compared to passively managed index funds. While capital gains are taxed at a lower rate than ordinary income, they still increase your overall tax liability. Passive funds, closely tracking a bond index, generally generate lower capital gains distributions, potentially resulting in a more tax-efficient outcome.

Tax-loss harvesting is another valuable strategy. This involves selling bond funds that have incurred a loss to offset capital gains realized in other parts of your portfolio. By carefully managing this strategy, you can reduce your overall tax liability. However, it's important to consult a financial advisor to understand the wash-sale rules and to ensure that tax-loss harvesting aligns with your long-term investment goals.

Finally, **strategic asset allocation** plays a crucial role in tax efficiency. By carefully diversifying across different bond types and fund structures, you can reduce your reliance on any single tax-sensitive investment, thereby mitigating potential tax burdens. A well-diversified portfolio, incorporating various bond categories and tax-advantaged options, can significantly improve your overall tax efficiency.

In conclusion, implementing tax-efficient strategies when investing in bond funds and ETFs requires careful consideration of several factors. By understanding the tax implications of different bond types, fund structures, and distribution policies, and by employing strategies like tax-loss harvesting and strategic asset allocation, investors can significantly reduce their tax liability and maximize their long-term investment returns. Seeking professional advice from a financial advisor can help you tailor a tax-efficient bond portfolio to meet your specific needs and financial goals.

17. Bond Funds and ETFs for Specific Financial Goals

College Savings

Planning for your child's college education is a significant financial undertaking, and understanding how bond funds and ETFs can play a role is crucial. While the allure of higher-return investments is tempting, the stability and relative predictability offered by bonds can provide a vital safety net within a diversified college savings portfolio. This section will explore how bond funds and ETFs contribute to a well-rounded approach to college savings, mitigating risk while aiming for consistent growth.

One of the key advantages of incorporating bonds into a college savings strategy is their *lower volatility* compared to stocks. The fluctuating nature of the stock market can be especially detrimental when saving for a long-term goal like college, as significant downturns could severely impact the overall savings accumulation. Bonds, with their generally lower risk profile, offer a degree of stability that can help cushion against market shocks. This is particularly important in the years leading up to college enrollment, where preserving capital is paramount.

Several types of bond funds and ETFs are well-suited for college savings, each offering a unique risk-reward profile. Short-term bond funds, for instance, are characterized by their shorter maturity dates, meaning less price fluctuation due to interest rate changes. These are excellent choices for those nearing the college enrollment timeframe, prioritizing capital preservation above high-growth potential. The lower risk associated with these funds comes at the cost of potentially lower returns compared to longer-term options.

Conversely, intermediate-term or long-term bond funds offer the potential for higher returns over longer horizons, making them attractive for parents starting to save earlier. While they carry slightly greater interest rate risk than their short-term counterparts, the increased potential returns can significantly enhance the savings over time. Careful consideration of the child's age and the anticipated college enrollment date is vital when choosing the appropriate duration of the bond fund.

Furthermore, the **tax implications** of various bond funds must be factored into the decision-making process. Municipal bond funds, for example, often offer tax-exempt income, which can significantly boost the overall returns for those in higher tax brackets. This tax advantage can substantially enhance the long-term growth of the college savings portfolio, making them a compelling option for many families. It is crucial to understand your state and local tax laws to maximize the benefit of tax-advantaged investments.

Beyond the fund type, investors should also consider the **management style**. Passive bond ETFs, which track a specific bond index, often come with lower expense ratios compared to actively managed bond funds. This translates into higher returns over time. However, actively managed funds offer the potential for outperformance if the fund manager makes shrewd investment decisions. The choice between passive and active management depends on individual risk tolerance and investment philosophy.

Successful college savings planning using bond funds and ETFs requires a <u>strategic approach</u>. Regular contributions, coupled with a diversified portfolio incorporating other asset classes (such as stocks), are key to maximizing growth while minimizing risks. A well-structured plan, tailored to the child's age and anticipated college expenses, is essential. Regular rebalancing of the portfolio ensures that the asset allocation remains aligned with the overall investment goals, helping to mitigate potential risks and maximize long-term growth.

In conclusion, integrating bond funds and ETFs into a college savings strategy offers a valuable tool for parents seeking to balance growth and risk mitigation. By carefully considering the various types of bonds, management styles, and tax implications, families can create a robust plan designed to secure their child's future education. The information provided here serves as a starting point, and seeking professional financial advice is always recommended to tailor a personalized college savings plan.

Down Payment Savings

Saving for a down payment on a home is a significant financial milestone, requiring careful planning and a strategic investment approach. While traditional savings accounts offer security, their low returns often fall short of the pace needed to accumulate a substantial down payment within a reasonable timeframe. This is where the versatility and potential of bond funds and ETFs can prove invaluable. By strategically incorporating these instruments into your savings plan, you can potentially accelerate your progress towards homeownership.

Understanding Your Time Horizon: The first step is determining your desired home purchase date. This dictates the timeframe you have for saving and influences your investment strategy. A shorter timeframe necessitates a more conservative approach, favoring short-term bond funds or ETFs for stability and capital preservation. Longer time horizons allow for greater risk tolerance, potentially incorporating a larger allocation to longer-term bond funds or even a small percentage of high-yield bond funds (depending on your risk profile) to boost potential returns. Remember, the key is balancing return potential against the risk of losing principal before your target purchase date.

Risk Tolerance and Investment Strategy: Your comfort level with risk is paramount. Individuals averse to risk will prioritize capital preservation, focusing on low-risk, investment-grade bond funds or ETFs that offer stability. These typically provide lower returns but minimize the chance of losing invested capital. Those with higher risk tolerance might consider a mix of investment-grade and high-yield options, but should carefully assess the potential for increased risk alongside higher potential returns. It's crucial to note that even high-yield bonds carry inherent risk, and it's important to understand that investments can decline in value.

Diversification for Stability: To mitigate risk, diversification is essential. A well-diversified portfolio would incorporate a range of bond types, potentially including government bonds, corporate bonds, and municipal bonds. Government bonds offer relative security and stability, corporate bonds provide exposure to the private sector's growth, and municipal bonds can offer tax advantages depending on your location and tax bracket. Utilizing ETFs allows for easy and cost-effective diversification across numerous bond holdings, offering a broader range of exposure.

Leveraging ETFs for Efficiency: Exchange-Traded Funds (ETFs) offer several advantages for down payment savings. Their low expense ratios compared to many actively managed bond funds translate into greater returns over time. The ease of trading and instantaneous pricing of ETFs makes them particularly suitable for those who may need to access a portion of their savings for unforeseen expenses while maintaining the potential for growth in the rest of their investment.

Monitoring and Adjustment: Regularly monitoring your portfolio's performance and adjusting your strategy as needed is crucial. As your target purchase date approaches, you may choose to shift your allocation towards more conservative, short-term bond instruments to minimize exposure to market fluctuations. Staying informed about market trends, economic conditions, and interest rate changes is crucial for making effective adjustments to your investment plan.

Professional Guidance: Considering the complexity of financial planning, consulting a qualified financial advisor is strongly recommended. A personalized plan will account for your specific financial situation, risk tolerance, and savings goals, providing tailored advice and investment guidance. They can help you make informed decisions and stay on track to achieve your down payment objectives effectively and efficiently.

In Conclusion: Bond funds and ETFs can significantly enhance your down payment savings journey. By carefully selecting a strategy that aligns with your timeline, risk profile, and financial goals, you can effectively accumulate the necessary capital for your dream home, potentially achieving this milestone sooner than you might expect through traditional savings methods alone. Remember, consistent saving, informed investment decisions, and seeking professional guidance are key ingredients to successful down payment savings.

Emergency Funds

Building a robust emergency fund is a cornerstone of sound personal finance, providing a crucial safety net against unexpected life events. While traditional savings accounts offer accessibility, they often fall short in terms of maximizing returns. This is where the strategic use of **bond funds and ETFs** can significantly enhance your emergency fund strategy.

Unlike stocks, which can experience significant volatility, *bonds generally offer greater stability*. This characteristic is particularly appealing for emergency funds, where the primary goal is capital preservation and readily available liquidity. Investing in **short-term bond funds or ETFs** provides a balance between safety and accessibility. These funds primarily hold bonds with maturities of less than one to three years, minimizing exposure to interest rate fluctuations and maximizing liquidity.

The *benefits of using bond funds for emergency funds are threefold*. First, they offer **diversification**. Instead of placing all your eggs in one basket (a single bond), a bond fund allows for diversification across numerous issuers and maturities. This reduces the risk associated with individual bond defaults. Second, they provide **easy access to your funds**. Most bond funds are easily traded, allowing you to quickly liquidate your assets when needed. Third, they offer **potentially higher returns** compared to traditional savings accounts. While not as high as stocks, the returns are usually better than those from low-yield savings accounts.

However, it's crucial to carefully consider the *specific characteristics of bond funds* when building your emergency fund. For instance, while short-term bond funds offer high liquidity, they might not generate substantial returns. **Investment-grade bond funds** generally carry lower risk but may offer lower yields than high-yield options. The decision of which type of bond fund to choose depends heavily on your individual risk tolerance and the size of your emergency fund. A more conservative approach might favor **government bond funds**, while those seeking slightly higher yields (while accepting a marginally higher risk) might consider **corporate bond funds** with high credit ratings.

Before investing in any bond fund or ETF, it's vital to *thoroughly research the fund's prospectus*, paying close attention to its expense ratio, past performance, and the types of bonds it holds. Compare different funds to find one that aligns with your financial goals and risk tolerance. Remember that even with the relative stability of bonds, **some level of risk always exists**, and the value of your investment may fluctuate. Therefore, regularly monitoring your emergency fund and adjusting your strategy as needed is recommended.

In conclusion, **bond funds and ETFs offer a compelling alternative to traditional savings accounts** for building an emergency fund. By carefully selecting short-term, investment-grade funds and understanding the associated risks, you can create a robust and accessible financial safety net to help navigate unexpected challenges.

Disclaimer: This information is for educational purposes only and should not be considered financial advice. Consult a qualified financial advisor before making any investment decisions.

18. The Future of Bond Funds and ETFs

Emerging Trends and Innovations

The world of bond funds and ETFs is dynamic, constantly evolving to meet the changing needs of investors and the broader financial landscape. Several key trends and innovations are reshaping how investors approach fixed-income investments. These advancements offer both opportunities and challenges, requiring investors to stay informed and adapt their strategies accordingly.

One significant trend is the rise of **factor-based investing** in the bond market. Traditional bond investing often focused on broad market indexes or actively managed strategies based on macroeconomic forecasts. Now, investors are increasingly using factor models to identify and target specific characteristics within bond portfolios, such as *quality*, *value*, and *momentum*. This allows for more targeted exposure to particular risk/reward profiles. For example, a quality factor might focus on bonds issued by companies with strong credit ratings and stable earnings, while a value factor might target undervalued bonds with potentially higher yields.

Another notable development is the growth of ESG (Environmental, Social, and Governance) investing in the bond market. Investors are increasingly incorporating ESG factors into their investment decisions, seeking to align their portfolios with their values and contribute to sustainable development. This involves analyzing the ESG performance of bond issuers and selecting bonds from companies with strong ESG profiles. The availability of ESG-focused bond ETFs and mutual funds is expanding rapidly, providing investors with diverse options for integrating sustainability into their fixed-income portfolios.

Technological advancements are also transforming the bond market. The use of big data analytics and artificial intelligence (AI) is enabling more sophisticated credit risk assessment and portfolio management. AI-powered platforms can analyze vast datasets to identify patterns and predict defaults, potentially leading to improved risk management and higher returns. Furthermore, blockchain technology holds the potential to streamline the bond issuance and trading processes, increasing efficiency and transparency. This could lead to the development of more innovative bond structures and potentially lower transaction costs.

The increasing popularity of exchange-traded notes (ETNs) is also a notable trend. While similar to ETFs, ETNs are debt instruments that track an underlying index but do not own the underlying assets. This can provide exposure to specific bond market segments or strategies at lower costs than traditional bond funds. Moreover, the introduction of fractional share investing is making bond funds and ETFs more accessible to retail investors, allowing them to invest in smaller increments and diversify their portfolios more effectively.

Finally, the growing sophistication of actively managed bond funds deserves mention. While passive strategies remain popular, active managers are increasingly using sophisticated quantitative models and alternative data sources to identify undervalued opportunities and generate alpha. This involves employing complex strategies such as arbitrage, relative value trading, and event-driven investing within the bond market, requiring specialized expertise and risk management capabilities.

In conclusion, the future of bond funds and ETFs is marked by innovation and rapid change. Investors need to actively monitor these trends, adapt their strategies, and consider the potential benefits and risks associated with these new approaches. Staying informed and seeking professional advice can help investors navigate this dynamic environment and maximize their returns while mitigating potential risks.

Impact of Technological Advancements

The financial landscape is undergoing a dramatic transformation, driven largely by **technological advancements**. This revolution profoundly impacts the world of bond funds and ETFs, reshaping how they are managed, accessed, and traded. This section explores the key ways technology is altering this investment arena.

One of the most significant impacts is the rise of *algorithmic trading*. Sophisticated algorithms now analyze vast datasets of market data, economic indicators, and even news sentiment to identify potential trading opportunities in the bond market with incredible speed and precision. This allows for **more efficient portfolio management** for both active and passive strategies. Active managers can use these algorithms to refine their trading strategies, while passive managers can achieve more precise index tracking. The automation also reduces the potential for human error, leading to potentially improved risk management.

Furthermore, <u>fintech platforms</u> are democratizing access to bond markets. Previously, investing in bonds, particularly in diverse portfolios of bonds, was often restricted to high-net-worth individuals and institutional investors. Now, through online brokerage platforms and robo-advisors, retail investors can access a wider range of bond funds and ETFs with **lower minimum investment requirements**. This increased accessibility fosters broader participation in the bond market, potentially leading to greater market efficiency and liquidity.

The **growth of big data and artificial intelligence (AI)** is another game-changer. AI-powered tools can analyze massive datasets to identify previously unseen patterns and trends, potentially improving credit risk assessment, forecasting interest rate movements, and optimizing portfolio construction. These tools can help both active and passive managers make more informed decisions, leading to potentially better risk-adjusted returns. The ability to process complex data rapidly and identify subtle relationships that would be impossible for human analysts to spot represents a significant advancement.

Blockchain technology holds the potential to revolutionize the efficiency and transparency of bond trading. By providing a secure and transparent record of bond transactions, blockchain could streamline the settlement process, reduce costs, and minimize the risk of fraud. This is particularly relevant for the bond market, which is often characterized by complex and opaque trading practices. While still in its early stages of adoption within the bond market, blockchain's potential for enhancing efficiency is substantial.

However, technological advancements also introduce **new challenges**. The increased reliance on algorithms raises concerns about potential biases in data and the possibility of algorithmic errors leading to market instability. Cybersecurity threats also pose a significant risk to the integrity of financial systems and data privacy. Careful consideration of these risks, along with robust regulatory frameworks, will be essential to mitigate potential downsides and ensure responsible innovation.

In conclusion, technological advancements are **reshaping the bond fund and ETF landscape** in profound ways. From algorithmic trading and fintech platforms to big data, AI, and blockchain, technology is increasing access, improving efficiency, and enhancing the sophistication of bond investing. However, addressing the associated risks and fostering responsible innovation is vital to ensure the continued growth and stability of this crucial part of the financial system.

Adapting to Market Changes

The dynamic nature of the bond market necessitates a proactive approach to investment strategies. Adapting to market changes is not merely a suggestion; it's a crucial element for successful long-term bond fund and ETF investing. This section explores the multifaceted challenges and opportunities presented by an ever-evolving landscape, focusing on how investors can maintain optimal portfolio performance.

One major challenge lies in interest rate fluctuations. Unpredictable shifts in interest rates can significantly impact bond prices. Long-term bonds are particularly vulnerable to rising rates, while short-term bonds offer relative stability but potentially lower returns. Sophisticated strategies, such as laddering maturities and barbell strategies, allow investors to mitigate interest rate risk by diversifying across various maturities. Furthermore, actively managed funds often employ sophisticated interest rate forecasting models to adjust portfolio composition in anticipation of rate changes. Staying informed on macroeconomic indicators and central bank policy announcements is essential for navigating this volatile aspect of the market.

Another key adaptation involves inflationary pressures. High inflation erodes the purchasing power of fixed-income investments. Investors need to incorporate inflation-protected securities (TIPS) into their portfolios to safeguard against this risk. The allocation to TIPS should be adjusted based on inflation forecasts and economic outlook, offering a hedge against potential price increases. Analyzing inflation indices and assessing the effectiveness of central bank measures in controlling inflation are vital steps in adapting investment strategies to this significant challenge.

The creditworthiness of issuers is another dynamic factor demanding attention. Credit ratings agencies constantly update their assessments, reflecting changes in the financial health of corporations and municipalities. Changes in credit ratings can drastically affect bond prices and yields. Investors should regularly monitor credit ratings and diversification across various credit quality levels. Actively managed funds have the flexibility to adjust credit exposure based on their assessment of credit risk. This requires careful monitoring of credit ratings and news regarding bond issuers to take prompt action when necessary.

The global macroeconomic environment plays a pivotal role in shaping bond market dynamics. Geopolitical events, economic slowdowns, or unexpected policy changes in different countries can all impact bond yields and prices. International bond funds, in particular, require a nuanced understanding of global economic conditions and currency fluctuations. Investors should carefully consider currency hedging strategies to mitigate the impact of exchange rate movements. A well-diversified portfolio that includes both domestic and international bonds can offer protection against unexpected global market shifts. Close monitoring of global economic indicators and political developments is indispensable.

Finally, technological advancements are reshaping the bond market. The rise of fintech and algorithmic trading is increasing market efficiency and creating new investment opportunities. Investors need to adapt by leveraging technology to access real-time data, enhance analytical capabilities, and streamline portfolio management. Understanding the implications of technological change for bond pricing, trading, and risk management is crucial. Staying updated on technological developments and adapting strategies accordingly are imperative to compete in this increasingly technological market.

In conclusion, successfully navigating the bond market requires a continuous process of learning and adaptation. By proactively monitoring key economic indicators, evaluating credit risks, adapting to changing interest rates, diversifying across different bond types and geographies, and leveraging technological advancements, investors can significantly enhance their chances of achieving long-term success in the dynamic world of bond funds and ETFs.

Printed in Great Britain
by Amazon

58445784R00088